THE BEST GUIDE FOR NONPROFIT CO

The Best Guide for Nonprofit Corporations

Including Churches & Religious Organizations

IMPORTANT NOTICE
The application FORM 1023 for 501C3 status has been updated. Please be sure you're using the October 2004 FORM 1023 located on The Best Guide For Nonprofits CD. You may also obtain the revised form at www.irs.gov or by calling 1-877-829-5500. Visit our website for updates and news at www.bestguidefornonprofits.com

THE BEST GUIDE FOR NONPROFIT CORPORATIONS

THE BEST GUIDE FOR NONPROFIT CORPORATIONS

DEDICATION

To my daughter, Adreanna, and my son, JaMarcus – never say these words to yourself: "I can't do it!" To my husband, Mario: Together we will move mountains. Thank you for making me so happy.

THE BEST GUIDE FOR NONPROFIT CORPORATIONS

ACKNOWLEDGMENTS

There are many people who have been an inspiration to me, so if I forget to put it on paper, I do thank you from the depths of my heart.

I would like to thank the people who believed in me the most, and seeded into my vision when I stared this journey. My daughter, Adreanna (at the age of 10), was the first one to donate $20. I hope you've learned something from me when it comes to sowing and reaping.

My mother, Doretha Simons, and my father, Joseph Simons, Jr., who always believed in me.

Stephanie Edmonds, Pat & Marylou Moore, Margaret Fick, Robert Edgar, Mike Miller, Heather Wirtz, Robert and Ada "Ruthie" Williams, Drs. Tom and Judith Weikel, Deborah Webb, and Beth Sturgeon.

Dr. Andrew and Mary Loyd for letting me do my first seminar at their church. Les Brown for motivating me to write the book. Bishop T.D. Jakes for letting me share my dream. And my best friend, Angela Corprew-Boyd.

IMPORTANT DISCLAIMER

This publication is intended to provide accurate and authoritative information with regard to the subject matter and should not be construed as legal advice or legal opinions. It is sold with the understanding that the publisher is not engaged in rendering legal or accounting services. If legal advice or assistance is required, the services of a competent professional person should be sought.

TABLE OF contents

INTRODUCTION

CHAPTER 1: What Is a Nonprofit Organization?..13

CHAPTER 2: Types of 501(C) Organizations 17

    Charitable..17

    Educational 18

    Religious...18

    Public Charities & Private Foundations 19

    Other 501(C) Status..20

CHAPTER 3: The Advantages of a Nonprofit Corporation................................23

    Tax Exemption 23

    The Right to Solicit Funds 24

    Grants 24

    Lower Postal Rates 26

    Unemployment Tax Exemptions..26

    Legal Life 26

    Employee Benefits 27

    Religious Organizations 27

CHAPTER 4: The Disadvantages of a Nonprofit Corporation 29

    Initial Out-of-Pocket Cost 29

    Legally Required Paperwork..29

    Small Operating Budget 30

    Getting Outsiders to 'Seed' into the Vision 31

CHAPTER 5: Step-by-Step Plan for Incorporating 33

    Step 1: Select a Name 33

    Step 2: Location for the Corporation 34

    Step 3: Purpose of the Corporation 34

    Step 4: Selecting Board Members 36

    Step 5: Registered Agent 37

    Step 6: Incorporators 38

    Step 7: Draft Articles of Incorporation 38

        (Sample) Articles of Incorporation for Individuals

        (Sample) Articles of Incorporation for a Church

        (Sample) Articles of Amendments

    Step 8: Draft a Set of Bylaws 55

        (Sample) Minutes of the Meeting

    Step 9: Submit Your Incorporating Document 65

    Step 10: You Are Official 65

CHAPTER 6: Applying for Tax-Exempt Status 67

    Record Keeping 68

    Filing Requirements 69

    Employee Identification Number (IRS Form SS-4) 70

    Application for Exemption (IRS Form 1023) 79

    IRS Form 872-C 101

    IRS Form 8718 121

    IRS Form 2848 123

    Checklist for Completing IRS Form 1023 125

    Where to Send Your Application 126

    State Fees, Addresses, Phone Numbers, and E-mail Addresses 126

CHAPTER 7: Tax Guide for Churches and Religious Organizations 135

    Tax-Exempt Status 139

Jeopardizing Tax-Exempt Status 142

Unrelated Business Income Tax (UBIT) 153

Employment Tax 156

Special Rules for Compensation of Ministers 158

Payment of Employee, Business Expenses..160

Record-Keeping Requirements 162

Filing Requirements 163

Charitable Contributions - Substantiation and Disclosure Rules 167

Special Rules Limiting IRS Authority to Audit a Church 168

Glossary 171

Help from the IRS 173

APPENDIX: Bylaws **177**

(Sample) Bylaws for Individuals

(Sample) Bylaws for a Religious Ministry or Church

INDEX **221**

THE BEST GUIDE FOR NONPROFIT CORPORATIONS

INTRODUCTION

This book was written with you in mind, to help make it simple, effective, and rewarding for you to complete your own application for exemption. Each section is designed with a "Tip" section to reference particular items you need to pay special attention to, or give just a little hint for you to remember when completing your application.

People often asked me how I began helping people start their own nonprofit corporations. It began when I had my own cake-decorating business in Norfolk, Va. I was in the military, and after I had my son, I decided to take a cake-decorating class so I could make my children's birthdays special. Three months later, I was in the third course for wedding cakes. After that, I decided I wanted to become an instructor. So I got in touch with the company, they put me in touch with the teacher coordinator, and she got me started. I began teaching and doing small cakes. My business grew so fast, the next thing I knew, I was doing wedding cakes. I entered cake shows, and received a lot of business from them. At these shows, I noticed the way different caterers put their food items on display. I love to see beautiful plate presentations. I began getting all kinds of cake-decorating books and cookbooks. It wasn't long before I found myself enrolled in Johnson & Wales University for Culinary Arts. It wasn't easy – we cooked 15-course meals twice a day. We ate a lot, did classroom work, and ate again. But I discovered something about myself: I didn't want to be a chef. I loved people and had a passion for helping others. So I said to myself, "One day I'm going to have my own culinary arts school for people who can't afford to pay almost $30,000 to go to Johnson & Wales."

After graduating from school, I moved to Orlando and got a job as food service director at a women's residential treatment facility. That's when I knew God was setting me up for something great. It wasn't long before I put together a curriculum and asked my director if I could teach the women culinary arts. She loved the idea because many of these women, age 18-50, had never cooked a meal before. The first class was a success, and very rewarding. That's when I got the idea to start my own nonprofit corporation. There weren't many lawyers who did this, and the ones who did charged fees that were outrageous. So I did the research and completed all the necessary steps to become a nonprofit corporation.

After some time, doing that birthed a new business. I started running into people who needed help getting their articles of incorporation and 501(C)(3) corporations started. I approached my pastor about conducting a seminar at the church, my desire was to empower people in teaching them how to do it themselves. Having faced a lack of funding, first for start-up costs, then for operating expenses to propel the organization and the vision in the right direction, I quickly recognized another need, one that would give me the opportunity to make a real difference. Working with a number of individuals, churches, schools, community service organizations, and other charitable groups enable us to collaborate our talents and abilities. God allowed me to use my talents and abilities, and then they would use theirs, thus *Multiplying Talents* was the only suitable name for my business. Today, I enjoy partnering with other businesses, conducting seminars.

Becoming an effective nonprofit organization takes time, patience, energy, money, and more money. Please don't be fooled about how easy it appears for other nonprofit organizations, whether a large church, school, daycare, or treatment facility. Believe me – they have paid their dues. They have learned what it takes to succeed. They have endured trials and tribulations. But the fact that they are still operating means basically one thing – they kept their eyes on the purpose, the mission, and the vision, and not on themselves.

One day I saw a church sign that read, "God did not call the qualified – He qualified the called." So I know that you were called to read this book, and I was called to write it to help you. Please help me multiply my talents by passing the book on to someone else.

CHAPTER ONE

What Is a Nonprofit Organization?

What do you want to be remembered for? After you are long gone, or even if you leave the corporation, the vision will still live on. Everybody in the world was sent here to "make a difference," to fulfill a purpose. And since you were given the vision, you were meant to make a difference.

Since you know that you're making a difference, hold yourself accountable, and surround yourself with people who will hold you accountable. It will be the best thing you can do for yourself and your corporation.

You have heard the term before, but do you really know what a *nonprofit organization* is? There are legal definitions, including 26 types of nonprofits recognized by the Internal Revenue Service (IRS). And there are common perceptions of what people mean when they refer to an organization as "nonprofit" or "not-for-profit". The IRS considers both terms to mean the same thing. Let's start with a definition:

A nonprofit is a tax-exempt organization that serves the public interest. In general, the purpose of this type of organization must be charitable, educational, scientific, or religious. This is a common and broad definition that fits the type of nonprofits explained in Chapter Two. The public expects to be able to make donations to these organizations and deduct these donations from their federal taxes.

Legally, a nonprofit organization is one that does not declare a profit. Instead, it utilizes all revenue available after normal operating expenses in service to the public interest. These organizations can be either unincorporated or incorporated. An unincorporated nonprofit cannot get federal tax-exempt status or the 501(C)(3) designation as defined by the IRS. When a nonprofit organization is incorporated, it shares many traits with for-profit corporations, except that there are no shareholders.

When starting a nonprofit corporation, an organization must file articles of incorporation with the state in which it resides, or the state it decides will be its jurisdiction for legal purposes. This is the same process a for-profit corporation must follow. Each state has various rules and regulations, but most require officers of the corporation, a board of directors, bylaws, and annual meetings. Most states also require nonprofit organizations to register with state charity bureaus or other agencies, and adhere to reporting requirements, particularly those involving fund-raising operations.

Nonprofit organizations have paid and volunteer staff, but employment taxes and federal and state workplace rules are generally no different from those imposed on for-profit organizations. A perception is that salaries in the nonprofit world are low, and while this is generally true, the type of nonprofit organization can make a huge difference in how closely its salary structure compares to the for-profit sector.

For example, universities, hospitals, and large national charities are organizations that can be "nonprofit" but have salary scales on a par with almost any for-profit corporation. CEOs of major hospitals commonly earn salaries and bonuses of $500,000 to more than $1,000,000. University presidents often have similar pay scales. However, local literacy training centers generally have lower salaries that are supplemented by payment in a smile from an adult who reads a first book.

A nonprofit organization can have clients, and can offer products and services, but needs revenue. Your corporation should market itself, and must be concerned with customer satisfaction, whether those "customers" are assisted or make donations in support of operations, programs, or services. It is a business that must serve the public interest, and it will succeed or fail as any business will, depending on how well it is operated.

Your Mission

Starting a charitable nonprofit can take you down many paths, but each journey begins with a single step and a *mission*. A mission is simply a clear statement of the scope and dimension of your nonprofit. Why does your nonprofit need to exist? Whom will it serve? What will it actually do? Where will you operate? The answers to these questions should help formulate a clear mission statement.

Once you know your mission, what are the technical issues of starting a nonprofit? First, you must determine if your mission requires establishing a nonprofit corporation. If you intend to raise funds in the form of tax-deductible contributions, the organization must serve some charitable, religious, educational, or scientific purpose beneficial to the public interest. This will allow the organization to seek tax-exempt status from the IRS, acquiring the designation of a 501(C)(3) charitable organization.

The designation "501(C)(3)" refers to the section of the U.S. Tax Code that deals with tax-exempt organizations. Tax-exempt organizations do not pay federal corporate income taxes. Not all state regulations are equal with regard to tax status of nonprofits, so be certain to check with your state government. Being designated a tax-exempt nonprofit also can qualify the organization for lower postal rates, and for government and private grants. (The negative part of incorporating is increased paperwork, recordkeeping, and reporting requirements.)

Incorporating as a nonprofit is similar to incorporating as a for-profit. Each nonprofit corporation must file articles of incorporation specifically stating the purpose of the organization. Each must establish bylaws, and consider regulations and operational requirements. And each state has independent regulations regarding incorporation.

Starting a nonprofit begins with a dream, grows with hope, and succeeds with hard but rewarding work. If you are up to the challenge, someone or something needs your commitment, concern, and passion. And you can make it happen.

CHAPTER TWO

Types of 501(C) Organization

There are 26 types of 501(C) organizations defined by the IRS. The most common types of 501(C)(3) organizations are charitable, educational, and religious. To be tax exempt, an organization must have one or more *exempt purposes* stated in its organizing document. Below are some definitions of the most commonly used exempt purposes.

CHARITABLE

Charitable organizations conduct activities that promote:

- relief of the poor, the distressed, or the underprivileged

- advancement of religion

- advancement of education or science

- erection or maintenance of public buildings, monuments, or works

- lessening the burdens of government

- lessening neighborhood tensions

- eliminating prejudice and discrimination

- defending human and civil rights secured by law

- combating community deterioration and juvenile delinquency

EDUCATIONAL

Educational organizations include:

- schools: primary, secondary, college or university, trade or professional school

- nonprofit day-care centers

- organizations that offer a "distance learning" course of instruction by correspondence or through television, radio, or the Internet

- organizations that conduct public discussion groups, forums, panels, lectures, or similar programs

- museums, zoos, planetariums, symphony orchestras, similar arts and educational organizations

- youth sports organizations

RELIGIOUS

According to the Internal Revenue Code (IRC), the term *church* includes synagogues, temples, mosques, and other similar types of religious organizations. The IRC excludes these organizations from the requirement to file an application for exemption. (Many churches voluntarily file them anyway.) This recognition by the IRS assures church leaders, members, and contributors that the church is tax-exempt under section 501(C)(3) and qualifies for related tax benefits. Other religious organizations that do not carry out the functions of a church may also qualify for exemption. These include mission organizations, nondenominational ministries, or faith-based social agencies. These organizations must apply for exemption from the IRS.

To be recognized as tax-exempt under section 501(C)(3) and eligible to receive tax-deductible contributions from the date of its creation, any organization other than a church, an integrated auxiliary of a church, or a convention or association of churches must file the application within 15 months from the end of the month in which it was created. But if an organization's annual gross receipts do not normally exceed $5,000, it is not subject to this 15-month rule.

The Difference between Public Charities and Private Foundations

Every organization that qualifies for tax-exempt status under IRC Section 501(C)(3) is further classified as either a *public charity* or a *private foundation*. Under IRC Section 508, every organization is automatically classified as a *private foundation* unless it meets one of the exceptions listed in Section 509(a).

Organizations that are classified as *public charities* under IRC Section 509(a) are:

- churches

- schools

- organizations that provide medical or hospital care, medical education, and, in certain cases, medical research

- organizations that receive a substantial part of their support in the form of contributions from publicly supported organizations, governmental units, and/or the general public

- organizations that normally receive not more than one-third of their support from gross investment income, and more than one-third of their support from contributions, membership fees, and gross receipts from activities related to their exempt functions

- organizations that support other public charities

If the organization requests public charity classification based on receiving support from the public, it must continue to seek significant and diversified public support in later years. A new organization that cannot show it has received enough public support may request an *advance ruling* of its status. At the end of its advance ruling period, usually five years, it must file a schedule showing its sources of support. If the schedule shows sufficient public support, the organization receives a definitive ruling of its *public charity* status. If the organization does not meet the public support requirements in the future, it could be reclassified as a *private foundation*. Unless the organization is committed to raising funds from the public, it may be more appropriate to consider alternate public charity classifications.

For some organizations, the primary distinction between a classification as a public charity or a private foundation is the *organization's source of financial support*. Generally, a public charity has a broad base of support while a private foundation has very limited sources of support. This classification is important because different tax rules apply to the operations of each. For one thing, deductibility of contributions to a private foundation is more limited than deductibility of contributions to a public charity. In addition, private foundations are subject to excise taxes that are not imposed on public charities. The special tax rules that apply to private foundations are covered in greater detail in Publication 578, *Tax Information for Private Foundations and Foundation Managers*.

Other 501(C) Status

As mentioned earlier, there are 26 classifications of 501(C) categories. Below is a list of a few of them. Check the definitions of each to make sure that you are filing the correct application for exemption.

501(C)(2) Title-Holding Corporation for Exempt Organization

501(C)(4) Civic Leagues, Social Welfare Organizations, and Local Associations of Employees

501(C)(5) Labor, Agricultural, and Horticultural Organizations

501(C)(6) Business Leagues, Chambers of Commerce, Real Estate Boards, and other business leagues

501(C)(7) Social and Recreation Clubs

501(C)(8) or 501(C)(10) Fraternal Beneficiary Societies and Domestic Fraternal Societies

501(C)(11) Teachers Retirement Fund Associations

501(C)(12) Local Benevolent Life Insurance Associations, Mutual Ditch or Irrigation Companies, Telephone Companies, and Similar Organizations

501(C)(13) Cemetery Companies

501(C)(14) State Chartered Credit Unions, Mutual Reserve Funds Organizations

501(C)(15) Mutual Insurance Companies and Associations

501(C)(16) Cooperative Organizations to Finance Operations

501(C)(17) Supplemental Unemployment Benefit Trusts

501(C)(19) Post or Organization of Past or Present Members of Armed Forces

501(C)(21) Black Lung Benefit Trusts

501(C)(22) Withdrawal Liability Payment Fund

501(C)(23) Veterans Organizations (created before 1880)

501(C)(25) Title-Holding Corporations or Trusts with Multiple Parents

501(C)(26) State-Sponsored Organizations Providing Health Coverage for High-Risk Health Individuals

501(C)(27) State-Sponsored Workers' Compensation Reinsurance Organizations

CHAPTER three

The Advantages of a Nonprofit Corporation

Originally, only people who had an excess amount of money started nonprofit corporations or foundations. However, today you'll see that parents, children, and even grandparents start their own nonprofit corporations with little money, but enjoying the same financial benefits as a for-profit business corporation. In this chapter, you'll read a brief description of the many advantages of starting a Nonprofit corporation.

Tax Exemption

One of the best benefits of being a 501(C)(3) nonprofit corporation is that your corporation is (a) exempt from paying federal corporate income tax; (b) exempt from paying state and local sales tax, property tax, and taxes on other assets (different states have different rules on property and assets taxes); (c) eligible for tax-deductible charitable contributions; and (d) exempt from certain employment taxes. Plus, individuals and corporate donors are more likely to support organizations with 501(C)(3) status because their donations can be tax-deductible.

An IRS determination of 501(C)(3) status is recognized and accepted for "other" purposes. For example: Because you are a nonprofit corporation, your state may grant you an exemption from state income tax, sales tax, and property tax. Contact your state's Secretary of State, Department of Revenue or tax office for details.

And it's not just your corporation that benefits – so do you. As an individual, you may deduct all your personal expenses every time you buy a stamp or a book for your business, every mile you drive, every trip you take, and every business phone call you make. No matter what you spend, you can write a certain percentage of those eligible expenses off your taxes on your 1040 Schedule A.

The Right to Solicit Donations

Unlike for-profit businesses, nonprofit corporations can solicit funds and other donations from many different individuals, corporations, foundations – the list goes on. Since you will more than likely rely heavily on public support financially, you will want to take advantage of being able to solicit funds. Businesses and individuals who donate like the fact that they get *tax-deductible* receipts for their hard-earned money.

You can also solicit non-monetary donations. Some business or individuals may prefer to donate things such as beautiful office furniture, computers, supplies, cars, homes, and media equipment – anything is possible.

Grants

501(C)(3) status qualifies your nonprofit corporation to receive a part of the billions of dollars in private and public grant money that is awarded out every year. If you are not recognized as a 501(C)(3) corporation, these foundations and philanthropy organizations will not even allow you to submit a grant request.

I've met many people who thought of an idea for a nonprofit corporation just for the purpose of getting grants. Please don't make this your focus for starting yours. Your 501(C)(3) is not an automatic grant magnet. However, recognition of exemptions under IRC section 501(C)(3) assures foundations and other grant-making institutions that the Nonprofit is using grants for sponsorship to permitted beneficiaries.

There are so many resources for funding your idea that you can spend hours online finding resources for grants proposals, how to apply for grants, foundations, and so on. If you're just getting started, you will be looking for grants that give "seed" money to help "initiate" your project. It's best to research sources that match what you are trying to do. Don't waste time reading information from a meat-packaging company when you are trying to fight animal abuse!

A grant is *usually* a one-time allocation of money given to a worthy cause. Finding someone to write a grant proposal should not be a problem. The problem may come when you find out how much it costs. It's best to offer a grant writer several hundred dollars to do the research, and give you the results, plus a commission of 1%-10% after you receive the grant. The percentage depends on the size of the grant. If the grant is for $5,000, then 10% is reasonable; if it's $1,000,000, then 1% is reasonable. This is just a guide. In any case, make sure you put it all in black and white in a signed contract.

 *TIP: Find out all the details and requirements of the grants or funds you are looking for – for example, what the funders are asking of your organization. They may ask you to do something that may not fit with your mission or religious beliefs, or that may add extra work to what you already have in mind. Funding sources usually want to see your organization's history of handling the kind of money you're asking for.*

You may be asking, "Well how can the organization get started if I don't have money to get it off the ground?" *Fundraising* is the key. Continuous fundraising. You need a steady stream of money coming in to keep your corporation active. It usually takes large corporations up to 18 months to give funds they have allocated for grants. You can always solicit smaller donations in the form of money, gifts certificates, merchandise, and so forth, from local stores and individuals as well as corporations.

Develop a relationship with your city officials. They know about funding that has been waiting for the right purpose. They need you, your ideas, and your resources to help make the community a better place. Check with your U.S. Senator's office: They know about funding legislation that has been passed in the Senate, and are supposed to take that information back to their constituents. Also call the office of your U.S. Representatives to Congress. These legislators have grant writers in their local offices that will help you by reading your grant requests to give you advice. They can't write it for you – they are just too busy for that. But they will help steer you in the right direction. Also, they can write "letters of support" for you, which will help when you need more documentation to support your mission or to become more effective. I once went to get help from my Congressman. His staff took special interest in my project, and two staff members asked me if they could be on my board of directors!

 *TIP: It's all about relationships. You must develop relationships with people in order to get what you need. Always be professional and courteous, and conduct yourself in a business like manner whenever you are dealing with the public. Actions speak louder than words.*

Lower Postal Rates for Bulk Mail

Everyone uses the U.S. Postal Service. And even though e-mail is everywhere, the postal system will be useful for years to come. A tax-exempt corporation can develop a mailing list from letters received, gift cards, personal postcards, invitations, tithes, and offerings. Before you know it, you will have at least 200 pieces of "real" mail to send. This puts you in the "bulk mailer" category, which means lower postage rates. In addition to paying postage, bulk mailers must get a mailing permit ($150 for each class of mail) plus pay an annual mailing fee ($150 a year for each class of mail).

There are many different rates for different classes of mail - first class, standard mail, advertisements, and such, and different quantities that must be mailed to get the lower postage rate. For example, the minimum number of pieces of standard mail is 200. Then letters cost 12.7 cents each to your own ZIP code, and 16.7 cents each outside your ZIP code. All you will need to have your tax-exempt letter to get approval. It generally takes a few weeks for the Post Office to process your paperwork.

 *TIP: Once you file your Articles of Incorporation, you will begin receiving all kinds of advertisements in the mail. One will be for the purchase of a postage meter. Do not purchase the meter if you do not have a large mailing list: That would be just another added expense that can wait.*

Unemployment Tax Exemptions

In some states, there are laws that involve state or unemployment compensation funds. As a nonprofit, you will not be required to contribute to payments that other employers are required to make. This would be a tremendous savings in your budget.

Legal Life

Once the IRS gives its definitive ruling, your corporation has a life of its own. It can even be treated as a "person." The corporation can receive loans, buy property, and conduct whatever business it has listed in the Articles of Incorporation. It can also be fined, but only the directors/founders can be charged and punished if found guilty of fraud or misuse. And the corporation can outlive you: After you're gone, your children can take over.

Employee Benefits

One the greater benefits a nonprofit corporation can offer its employees and officers is health and life insurance. A nonprofit corporation can also establish a pension plan, or retirement plan. Each of these plans may require some cost contribution from employees, as in most businesses, so that the burden isn't entirely on the corporation.

Religious Organizations

A church may obtain recognition of exemption for any or all periods prior to the time it asks that the IRS make a determination as to its tax-exempt status. Many churches don't have their 501(C)(3) in place because they don't want to be audited by the IRS. Even if you aren't an approved 501(C)(3) organization, you are still subject to the laws of the land. And being an approved 501(C)(3) will only protect your church. But applying for 501(C)(3) status benefits a church in many ways. From my experience in helping churches apply for 501(C)(3), I have seen churches grow because they became more serious about their integrity and their mission.

If a church has a "parent," which means it's under the umbrella of another church that is tax-exempt, the parent may have a "group exemption letter." If it does, then the organization seeking exemption may already be recognized as exempt by the IRS. Under the group exemption process, the parent organization becomes the holder of a group exemption ruling naming other affiliated churches as being included within the ruling. This means that a church is recognized as exempt if it is included in the annual update of the parent organization. If the church is included on such a list, no further action is needed for obtaining this recognition.

There's a difference between a church and a ministry. A church is defined as an established place of worship, and a ministry simply could be someone who travels for speaking engagements or preaching. Some churches have now decided to call themselves "ministries" instead, but if you have an established place of worship and you conduct regular Sunday services, Sunday school, or whatever, then you are considered a church for IRS purposes.

 *TIP: Many people have come to me to attempt to file their application for exemption, but still have their churches in their homes. That is okay to start with, but the IRS prohibits you from taking tithes and offerings in your home because you could be using it to pay your rent, and not on the building that will be used as a public place of worship. If you are starting a ministry or a church, you cannot apply for a 501(C)(3) until you have an established place with a physical address. The IRS will require a copy of the purchase agreement or a lease. See Schedule A (for a Church) on Form 1023.*

CHAPTER four

The Disadvantages of a Nonprofit Corporation

After reading some of the advantages, you may see yourself starting immediately, and there's no reason why you shouldn't. However, there are some disadvantages that you should be aware of, and, hopefully, knowing some of the disadvantages may better prepare you for your business.

Initial Out-of-Pocket Cost

This is the one problem many people may encounter. You are doing all the work and forking over all the money to get the corporation started. But doing it yourself keeps your out-of-pocket expenses low, compared to hiring someone to do the paperwork, and even better than getting a loan for starting a for-profit business. You are saving yourself hundreds, possibly thousands, of dollars. Some of those expenses may be:

- business cards and stationery

- phone line

- office supplies

- equipment, office furnishings

- Advertising

- Bank charges

- Postage fees

Legally Required Paperwork

Keeping your corporation active will require you to pay annual fees, and pay them on time to avoid penalty fees. State tax collectors and the IRS are notorious for adding late charges. Some states also require additional fees: Contact your state for a complete list of fees required. Once you are an approved 501(C)(3) entity, you will not pay any annual fees to the IRS. But if you are required to file a Form 990 and you fail to do so by the due date, you will have to pay a penalty. See the Appendix section for the forms you need to cover the legally required paperwork and start-up requirements.

Small Operating Budget

Many people have started nonprofit corporations, made their way through the incorporation process and the 501(C)(3) process, received a few monetary donations and maybe a grant, but didn't know what it takes to keep the nonprofit corporation running.

What about a staff? Someone has to do the work. You can't do all the work by yourself – at least not for long. Do you need a staff? Can you pay a staff? Can you recruit and retain volunteers? Workers are needed for two general responsibilities: administrative and service. Administrative workers run the corporation, including raising funds, managing budgets, and handling all business operations. Service workers are responsible for the mission of the organization, and for accomplishing the purpose for which the nonprofit was formed. In small nonprofits, one staff member may do it all. This is where volunteers become critical to the success of the nonprofit.

What about the budget? Where will funding come from? Nonprofits earn income through program and service fees, but raising funds is usually an essential activity. Fundraising is simply the result of matching a compelling cause or need with a philanthropically minded individual, organization, or company. Philanthropy is a massive industry in the United States; more than $212 billion was donated in 2001, according to *Giving USA*. The key to successful fundraising is asking. It may seem simplistic, but most people fear talking about or *asking* for money. Do not wait for donors to come to you. Ask and you shall receive – most of the time.

The one key to keeping the business going is to do fundraisers on a frequent basis. Even if you have met your budget for the year, you need several constant streams of income. If you work full-time, you may want to put 10% of your pay into your nonprofit if you are brand new. If you have been operating for a few years and your funds are low, you still may want to contribute part of your pay. The key is not to wait for or depend on grants. Instead, have your board of directors constantly work on fund-raising ideas – then put them into action.

Getting Outsiders to 'Seed' into the Vision

It seems people find it hard to give to a new organization. They want to donate only to a familiar "sure thing" like the YMCA or a hospital, not a new nonprofit. An outsider is someone who doesn't know you or trust you yet. They're "outsiders," and you need to bring them in. That's why, especially when you're first starting out, you have to build relationships with all kinds of people: teachers, nurses, clergy, business owners, athletic coaches, and many others. You never know who knows whom, and who will be able to help you. Your job is to take every opportunity to talk about what you're doing and what you need to keep doing it. You want these people to contribute, to "seed" into the vision to help you make it grow.

When I first started, I told people about my vision for a nonprofit corporation, and many of them contributed to it. My first donation came from my daughter. The next came from a family I had just met through a good friend.

If, however, you do not receive enough funding to provide for all of your operational and service needs, consider partnering with a similar organization. A trend in the nonprofit industry is sharing resources that are common to many nonprofits. This could take the form of sharing office space, administrative tasks, fund raising, and other work that a small nonprofit may need but not to the extent of requiring a full-time employee. You may be able to partner with an organization that could use the services you provide within the scope of their larger mission. Research your local nonprofit community to determine if a similar organization exists, and if your services would be complementary to their mission.

CHAPTER five

Step-by-Step Plan for Incorporating

Completing the legal requirements for incorporating is fairly simple because your particular state has a guide for you to go by. However, going to the next level of completing your tax-exempt application with the IRS will require an extra step in creating your incorporating documents. The details will be found later in this chapter.

If you want to start from scratch by typing the incorporating document, type on standard or legal-size white typing paper. Use the IRS language provided, and insert any clause that applies to your corporation.

STEP 1: SELECT A NAME

Selecting a name was probably the first thing you did, before you thought about anything else. The name of your corporation is very important, as it sometimes identifies your business; for example, ABC Carpet Cleaning, Inc. The name sometimes reflects the purpose of your business; for example, The New Church, Inc. Once you file your Articles of Incorporation, the name you choose will be recorded for your organization. After getting your Certificate of Incorporation from the state, make sure you put your name on every document exactly as it appears on the original articles. Failure to do so will cause the IRS to return your paperwork.

A corporate name is the name of a filed business entity. Before your corporate name is registered, the state checks to be sure it isn't taken and that it's unique and is checked for distinguishability for state records. The exact name will not be granted to another business entity. A *fictitious name* is only a registration of your name, required for "notice" purposes to the public. There are no ownership rights in a fictitious name, and the name is not protected against use by anyone else. The same fictitious name can be used repetitively.

Go to your state's Web site to make sure the name you want has not already been selected. If it has, you might be able to add a word to change the name. Filing a Fictitious Name application costs money, but they are easy enough to do yourself. Consult with your individual state's office.

You may apply for your Articles of Incorporation online on some states Web sites; however, there is limited space to type and there are several IRS clauses that must be written in your articles to be approved by the IRS.

TIP: The law restricts the use of certain names that may be offensive or distasteful, or any name that is misleading. For example, if you state that you will operate as a foundation, credit union, or labor union, but you have no intention or ability to operate as such. The use of a person's name (other than your own) is restricted by law.

STEP 2: LOCATION FOR THE CORPORATION

The location of your business may be obvious by the state you file your application in, but some corporations want to be nationwide. If that is the case, then you must register in each state and abide by that state's laws, rules, and regulations. However, your principal office must have one location from which it conducts activities. You may use your home address or (in some states) a post office box number. But for the official record, you should use a street address for the principal office of the corporation.

TIP: If you plan to operate a church, you must have an established place of worship. As a 501(C) entity, you may conduct Bible study in your home, but once you establish your corporation, you must have an official place of worship. You can use your home address for correspondence purposes only.

STEP 3: PURPOSE OF THE ORGANIZATION

When typing your Articles of Incorporation, your purpose can be as simple or as detailed as you'd like it to be, but the IRS requires certain language and disclaimers to be stated in your articles and bylaws. For example, your purpose may be:

To conduct a culinary art training program for welfare-to-work recipients.

Or

To conduct a local church by the direction of the Lord Jesus Christ and under the leadership of the Holy Spirit in accordance with all of the commandments and provisions as set forth in the Holy Bible.

Since you're applying for tax exempt status, this IRS language must be added to your purpose:

The corporation is organized exclusively for charitable, religious, and educational purposes, including, for such purposes, the making of distributions to organizations that qualify as exempt organizations under section 501(C)(3) of the Internal Revenue Code, or the corresponding section of any future federal tax code.

No part of the net earnings of the corporation shall inure to the benefit of, or be distributable to its members, trustees, officers, or other private persons, except that the corporation shall be authorized and empowered to pay reasonable compensation for services rendered and to make payments and distributions in furtherance of the purposes set forth in Article (insert your article number that your purpose is stated in) *hereof.*

Upon the dissolution of the Corporation, the Board of Directors shall, after paying or adequately providing for all the debts, obligations, and liabilities of the Corporation, distribute the remaining assets of the Corporation exclusively for the nonprofit religious purposes to such organization or organizations which are tax exempt under section 501(C)(3) of the Code, as amended, as the Board of Directors in its sole discretion shall determine.

The extent of personal liability, if any, for directors, officers, or members for corporate obligations and the methods of enforcement and collection, are as follows: NONE. Further, the Directors and officers shall be exempt from liability and/or indemnified from costs and judgments to the full extent permitted by Florida law. In the event the (your state) *law is subsequently amended to authorize the further elimination or limitation of the liability of Directors or Officers of nonprofit corporations, then the liability of Directors and Officers of the corporation in addition to the limitation on person liability provided under this Article, shall be limited to the fullest extent permitted by such later amended* (your state name) *law.*

 *TIP: If you don't add these statements, the IRS will return your application to you, to include these statements. In effect, it will delay your application, because you will also have to amend your state application, plus pay an amendment fee. Then wait for your state to return your Organization Documents.*

These statements consist of a promise to expend all of the corporation's available resources in furthering its nonprofit goal, and a disclaimer of any intent by the corporation's members, directors, or officers to earn a profit. It is also pledges that if the corporation is ever dissolved, all assets and funds remaining after the corporation's operating expenses have been paid will be passed on to other organizations devoted solely to nonprofit purposes.

STEP 4: YOUR BOARD MEMBERS

The corporation's board of directors will have the right to vote on any matters concerning the corporation. Voting rights should be established in the Bylaws of the Corporation. Congress has mandated that each board member be an adult citizen of the United States. Some states only require that you have only three incorporators (persons who form the corporation) and/or three directors. The incorporators may also be named as the directors, so one person (including yourself) can act as a member of the board of directors or as incorporator. Some states don't use the term incorporator, just board of directors, so please don't get confused. The attached sample Articles of Incorporation uses both, and you may omit the term that doesn't conform to your state laws.

One of your board's jobs is to come up with fund-raising ideas, put them into effect, and keep the corporation healthy financially. You need a diverse group of people on your board of directors, people who (1) know how to get money and aren't afraid to go get it, or (2) have money and aren't too stingy to give it. Your board of directors should be people who believe in your vision, people you trust with your reputation. The number of people you have should be an odd number so that whenever there's a vote on something, you'll have a tie breaker. Five or seven members is good to start with, and you can always have more people who are willing to serve as a *board of advisors* but have no decision-making power.

In the many seminars I've presented, the biggest problem I see for most new corporations has to do with the function of the board of directors. The directors don't know their roles and are not effective for the corporation because people are in such a rush to get the 501(C)(3) approved that they will name the husband or wife and a child or relative as the board of directors.

I've also encountered people who have filled out their 501(C)(3) application, gotten a negative response from the IRS, and then asked me for help. After looking at their paperwork, I could see that the individuals on their board were no help to them financially, emotionally, or physically. Naming too many family members to your board of directors usually raises a red flag because it's too much control in one family, and may cause a conflict of interest. It may also be misinterpreted when you seek grants or other funds.

Your state may send you an annual Uniform Business Report (UBR) that will ask you for any additions or deletions you may have. At that time, you may change your original board of directors. Normally, the original board will serve at least the first year of operation.

TIP: For corporations just starting, if your nonprofit corporation expects to receive tax-exempt status from the IRS, its bylaws should also state that the directors or board members do not receive regular salaries. But you can pay them reasonable fees for services (for examples travel reimbursement) or for expenses they may incur for attending meetings of the board.

If your corporation will be structured as a private foundation, you should know that, strictly in a tax sense, the IRS will identify certain persons involved in the corporation as *disqualified persons*. A disqualified person is someone who has contributed more than $5,000 to the corporation, if that amount equals more than 2% of the total contributions made in the same tax year.

TIP: Your board of directors needs to know that being on the board is not just about power – it's about responsibility: to the corporation, its members, and its mission. A good deal of responsibility comes with being a board member. Make sure the people you choose are responsible in their personal affairs, so that they don't become a burden to the organization or its purpose.

STEP 5: REGISTERED AGENT

All documents pertaining to the corporation are forwarded to the registered agent. The registered agent acts on behalf of the corporation to handle the necessary paperwork. The agent is not financially responsible for the corporation. Lawyers are often agents for corporations. In most states, the incorporator can also act as the agent.

STEP 6: INCORPORATORS

Incorporators are the people who formed the corporation. The names, addresses, and titles should be listed on the corporation's articles.

STEP 7: DRAFT ARTICLES OF INCORPORATION

A corporation is formed by the filing of Articles of Incorporation with the state, and the state date-stamps the articles before they become effective. It's a good idea to check the laws of the state in which the organization is incorporated.

Each state has its own forms for incorporating, but usually has only the *minimum* requirements for incorporating on the application. Because they see so many applications every day, they want the minimum requirements from you. You will be mailing a copy of these Articles of Incorporation with your application for your 501(C)(3), and the IRS will require additional statements which are explained in this chapter.

Each state has different requirements and fees. The Florida Articles of Incorporation application is different from South Carolina's. (See the list of names, addresses, Web sites, and cost to incorporate in the back of this book.)

A corporation with business locations in multiple states will typically incorporate in a single state, then "qualify to do business" in the other states. This means they formally register in these other states, paying additional taxes and filing annual reports, as required. However, you must keep track of everything, or filing-fee penalties can hurt your pocketbook.

THE BEST GUIDE FOR NONPROFIT CORPORATIONS

SAMPLE ARTICLES OF INCORPORATION OF A NONRELIGIOUS CORPORATION

ARTICLES OF INCORPORATION

OF

_____, INC.

(Insert your corporation name here)

The undersigned, a majority of whom are citizens of the United States, desiring to form a Nonprofit Corporation under the Nonprofit Corporation Law of Florida, do hereby certify:

FIRST: The name of said corporation shall be _____, Inc.

SECOND: The place in Florida where the principal office of the corporation is to be located at _____, FL. (address, city)

THIRD: The purposes for which said corporation is formed are:

(A) To receive and maintain real or personal property, or both and subject to the restrictions and limitations hereinafter set forth, to use and apply the whole or any part of the income and the principal thereof exclusively for charitable, religious, and educational purposes either directly or by contributions to organizations that qualify as exempt organizations under Section 501(C)(3) of the IRC code and its regulations as they now exist or they may hereafter be amended. More specifically, these purposes shall include but are not limited to:

(1) To maintain a residential or halfway house for rehabilitating young adults between the ages 18-25 years old, that have problems such as marriage, personal, alcohol and drug abuse.

(2) To motivate young adults to live victorious lives through meetings, recreation, and Christian teaching and instruction.

(3) To promote moral character and self-esteem among the youth and adults.

(4) To combat juvenile delinquency and adult illiteracy.

(B) No part of the net earnings of the corporation shall inure to the benefit of, or be distributable to its members, trustees, officers, or other private persons, except that the corporation shall be authorized and empowered to pay reasonable compensation for services rendered and to make payments and distributions in furtherance of the purposes set forth in Article Three hereof.

(C) Upon the dissolution of the Corporation, the Board of Directors shall, after paying or adequately providing for all the debts, obligations, and liabilities of the Corporation, distribute the remaining assets of the Corporation exclusively for the nonprofit religious purposes to such organization or organizations which are tax exempt under section 501(C)(3) of the Code, as amended, as the Board of Directors in its sole discretion shall determine. The extent of personal liability, if any, for directors, officers, or members for corporate obligations and the methods of enforcement and collection, are as follows: NONE. Further, the Directors and Officers shall be exempt from liability and/or indemnified from costs and judgments to the full extent permitted by Florida law. In the event the (Florida) law is subsequently amended to authorize the further elimination or limitation of the liability of Directors or Officers of nonprofit corporations, then the liability of Directors and Officers of the corporation in addition to the limitation on personal liability provided under this Article, shall be limited to the fullest extent permitted by such later amended Florida law.

FOURTH: The following persons shall serve said corporation as Board of Directors until the first annual meeting.

Name   Address

_____   _____

_____   _____

_____   _____

FIFTH: No drugs or alcoholic beverages shall at any time be permitted upon any property owned by the corporation.

SIXTH: The registered agent's name and address is _____

_____ _____
Registered Agent Signature   Date

_____ _____
Registered Agent Signature   Date

THE BEST GUIDE FOR NONPROFIT CORPORATIONS

SAMPLE ARTICLES OF INCORPORATION FOR A RELIGIOUS CORPORATION

ARTICLES OF INCORPORATION

OF

_____, INC.

(Insert your corporation name here)

The undersigned, a majority of whom are citizens of the United States, desiring to form a Nonprofit Corporation under the Nonprofit Corporation Law of Florida, do hereby certify:

ARTICLE I

CORPORATION NAME

The name of the Corporation shall be _____ Ministry, Inc.

ARTICLE II

DURATION

The period of duration of this Corporation is perpetual, unless dissolved according to law. Corporate existence shall commence upon the filing of these Articles of Incorporation.

ARTICLE III

CORPORATE PURPOSES: POWERS

1. The purpose for which the Corporation is organized and operated purpose/is exclusively for charitable, religious, educational, and scientific purposes, including, for such purposes, the making of distributions to organizations that qualify as exempt organizations under section 501(C)(3) of the Internal Revenue Code, or the corresponding section of any future federal

tax code. Such purposes shall include the following:

(a) Religious

(b) To conduct a local Church by the direction of the Lord Jesus Christ and under the leadership of the Holy Spirit in accordance with all of the Commandments and provisions as set forth in the Holy Bible, the irrevocable Word of God. Pursuant thereto, the following activities and guidelines shall be established.

　　i. A recognized creed, code of doctrine, discipline and form of worship shall be established.

　　ii. An ecclesiastical form of government shall be established.

　　iii. Ordination of ministers upon completion of the prescribed course of study, designated by this Church Ministry.

　　iv. An organization of ministers shall be established to minister to the congregation of the Church.

　　v. Establishment of a Church membership based upon acceptance of a recognized creed and belief and support of the Church.

　　vi. Establishment of various religious services pursuant to the recognized creed, form of worship, code of doctrine and discipline of the Church literature, and other forms of mass media for the purpose of educating the individual in the Word of God.

　　vii. Establishing a school for the preparation of ministers who minister to the Church.

(c) Minister the Word of God to the faithful.

(d) Promote and encourage, through the ministry of the organization, cooperation with other organizations, ministering within the community.

(e) To acquire and hold such property, either real or personal, for Church purposes, as may be necessary for its membership and the worship of God.

2. As a means of accomplishing the above purposes and methods, the Corporation shall have the following powers:

(a) To receive and accept gifts of money and property and to hold the same for any of the purposes of the Corporation and its work.

(b) To raise and assist in raising funds for the purposes herein set forth, including the issuance of bonds or other instruments of credit.

(c) To acquire, own, lease, mortgage, and dispose of property both real and personal.

(d) To conduct and carry on religious services and instruction through the public media, including electronic broadcasting, AM and FM radio, telecasting, microwave distribution, closed circuit transmission, and cable television.

(e) To accept property and donations in trust for religious or charitable purposes.

(f) To acquire, hold, own, sell, assign, transfer, mortgage, pledge, or otherwise dispose of shares of the capital stock, bonds, obligations, or other securities of other corporations, domestic or foreign, as investment or otherwise, in carrying out any of the purposes of the Corporation and, while the owner thereof, to exercise all rights, powers, and privileges of ownership, including the power to vote thereon.

(3) The property of the Corporation is irrevocably dedicated to religious, educational, and charitable purposes, and no part of the net earnings of the corporation/organization shall inure to the benefit of, or be distributable to, its members, trustees, directors, officers, or other private persons, except that the corporation/organization shall be authorized and empowered to pay reasonable compensation for services rendered and to make payments and distributions in furtherance of Section 501(C)(3) purposes.

(a) No substantial part of the activities of the corporation/organization shall be the carrying on of propaganda, or otherwise attempting to influence legislation, and the corporation/organization shall not participate in, or intervene in (including the publishing or distribution of statements) any political campaign on behalf of, or in opposition to, any candidate for public office.

(b) The Corporation shall not:

i. Operate for the purpose of carrying on a trade or business for profit;

ii. Accumulate income, invest income, or divert income, in a manner endangering its exempt status; or

    iii.   Except to an insubstantial degree, engage in any activity or exercise any powers that are not in furtherance of the purposes of the Corporation.

    iv.   The Corporation's operations are to be conducted principally in the United States of America.

ARTICLE IV

REGISTERED OFFICE AND AGENT

The initial street address and mailing address of the principal office and registered office of the Corporation is: 1234 Beacon Lane, Orlando, FL 32868, and the name of registered agent at such address is Susan Bell.

ARTICLE V

MANAGEMENT OF CORPORATE AFFAIRS

The powers of the Corporation shall be exercised by or under the authority of, and the business and affairs of the Corporation shall be managed under the directions of, a Board of Directors which shall have three (3) directors initially. The number of directors may be increased or decreased from time to time by a majority of the directors, but at no time shall there be fewer than three (3) directors of the Corporation.

ARTICLE VI

INITIAL DIRECTORS

The manner in which the Directors of the Corporation shall be elected or appointed shall be governed by the provisions of the Bylaws of the Corporation. The names and street addresses of the initial directors of the Corporation are:

Name   Street Address

_____   _____

_____   _____

_____   _____

ARTICLE VII

CORPORATE NATURE

The Corporation is organized under a non-stock basis.

ARTICLE VIII

MEMBERS

This Corporation shall have members and they shall be admitted and qualified in accordance with the Bylaws adopted by the Board of Directors.

ARTICLE IX

AMENDMENTS

Amendments to these Articles of Incorporation may be adopted by a majority of the directors in the manner set forth in the Bylaws of this Corporation.

ARTICLE X

INCORPORATOR

The name and address of the Incorporator is: Susan Bell, 1234 Beacon Lane, Orlando, FL 32868

ARTICLE XI

MISCELLANEOUS

(a) Notwithstanding any other provision of these articles, the corporation/organization shall not carry on any other activities nor permitted to be carried on:

  i. By a corporation/organization exempt from Federal income tax under Section 501(C)(3) of the IRC (or corresponding section of the any future Federal tax code) or

  ii. By a corporation/organization, contributions to which are deductible under Section 170(C)(2) of the IRC (or corresponding section of any future Federal tax code.)

(b) Upon dissolution of this corporation/organization, assets shall be distributed for one or more exempt purposes within the meaning of Section 501(c)(3) of the Internal Revenue Code, or corresponding section of any future Federal tax code, or shall be distributed to the Federal government, or to a state or local government, for a public purpose.

Dated this 21st day of July, 2_____.

IN WITNESS WHEREOF, the undersigned Incorporator has executed these Articles of Incorporation.

_____

Susan Bell, Incorporator, President

Articles of Amendments

If you have already completed your articles of incorporation and they do not have the IRS language, then you will need to file an Article of Amendment to change your original articles to comply with the IRS requirements. No matter what minimum requirements your state has for incorporating, there are still certain disclaimer statements (located in the Tip section under Step 3), that must be in your articles. A "conformed copy" is a copy that agrees with the original Articles of Incorporation and all of its amendments. If the original document required a signature, the copy should be signed by a principal officer or accompanied by a written declaration signed by an authorized officer. With either option, the officer must certify that the document is a complete and accurate copy of the original.

THE BEST GUIDE FOR NONPROFIT CORPORATIONS

SAMPLE ARTICLES OF AMENDMENT

ARTICLES OF AMENDMENT

TO

ARTICLES OF INCORPORATION

OF

<u>THE REAL COOKING SCHOOL, INC.</u>
present name

NO10000004444
Document Number of Corporation

Pursuant to the provisions of section 617.1006, Florida Statues, the undersigned Florida nonprofit corporation adopts the following Articles of Amendments to its Articles of Incorporation.

First: Amendment(s) adopted: Article I being amended, Article III and V being added to previous articles.

ARTICLE I

The name of this corporation shall be THE COOKING SCHOOL, Inc.

ARTICLE III

The corporation is organized exclusively for charitable, religious, and educational purposes, including, for such purposes, the making of distributions to organizations that qualify as exempt organizations under section 501(C)(3) of the Internal Revenue Code, or the corresponding section of any future federal tax code.

ARTICLE V

No part of the net earnings of the corporation shall inure to the benefit of, or be distributable to, its members, trustees, officers, or other private persons, except that the corporation shall be authorized and empowered to pay reasonable compensation for services rendered and to make payments and distributions in furtherance of the purposes set forth in Article Three hereof.

Upon the dissolution of the Corporation, the Board of Directors shall, after paying or adequately providing for all the debts, obligations, and liabilities of the Corporation, distribute the remaining assets of the Corporation exclusively for the nonprofit religious purposes to such organization or organizations which are tax exempt under section 501(C)(3) of the Code, as amended, as the Board of Directors in its sole discretion shall determine.

The extent of personal liability, if any, for directors, officers, or members for corporate obligations and the methods of enforcement and collection, are as follows: NONE. Further, the Directors and Officers shall be exempt from liability and/or indemnified from costs and judgments to the full extent permitted by Florida law. In the event Florida law is subsequently amended to authorize the further elimination or limitation of the liability of Directors or Officers of nonprofit corporations, then the liability of Directors and Officers of the corporation in addition to the limitation on personal liability provided under this Article, shall be limited to the fullest extent permitted by such later amended Florida law.

Second: The date of adoption of the amendment(s) was: <u>February 2, 2000</u>

Third: Adoption of Amendment – There are no members entitled to vote on the amendment. The amendments were adopted by the Board of Directors.

_____

Signature of the President

Typed Name

_____   _____
President   Date

_____   _____
Title   Date

THE BEST GUIDE FOR NONPROFIT CORPORATIONS

STEP 8: DRAFT A SET OF BYLAWS

You need bylaws! Bylaws should be established in the beginning as a guide to how the organization will be run. Some states do not require them, but most corporations have them for their protection and benefit. You can make any rules you want into your bylaws, as long as they don't violate the state's nonprofit incorporation laws. Bylaws are simple rules and regulations that tell the directors and the public how your corporation is operated from a business perspective. Even though it is a nonprofit corporation, it's still a business, and the corporation should be treated as such.

Acceptable bylaws should include:

1. Organizational name exactly as it appears in the organizational document (Articles)
2. Purposes
3. Classes of membership and the qualifications for each class
4. How and by whom the affairs of the organization will be administered
5. Officers, and the duties of each officer
6. Meetings (how often held)
7. Fiscal year of the organization
8. Provisions for making amendments to the bylaws and Certificate of Incorporation
9. The date the bylaws were adopted
10. Provisions for elections of officers

Lastly, the bylaws should be signed by the officers of the organization, and dated.

You should also have a statement in your bylaws that allows for changes to me made.

The bylaws on the following pages show you how your bylaws should read. After that is a list of religious organization bylaws. You can add items that are relevant to your own corporation.

SEE APPENDIX FOR SAMPLE BYLAWS

THE BEST GUIDE FOR NONPROFIT CORPORATIONS

Acceptable Bylaws for a Religious Organization Should Include:

1. Organizational name and address exactly as it appears in the Articles of Incorporation.

2. Statement of Faith

3. A Creed and form of worship

4. A definite and distinct ecclesiastical government

5. Classes of membership and the qualifications for each class

6. Voting Rights of Membership

7. Church Officers and the duties of each officer

8. How and by whom the affairs of the organization will be administered

9. Meeting (how often held)

10. Elected Church Officers

11. Committees and Coordinating Groups

12. Program Organizations (for example, Sunday School, music programs)

13. Fiscal year of the organization

14. Provisions for making amendments to the bylaws and Certificate of Incorporation

15. Date the bylaws were adopted

16. Provisions for elections of officers

Bylaws should be signed and dated by the officers of the organization.

SEE APPENDIX FOR SAMPLE BYLAWS

THE BEST GUIDE FOR NONPROFIT CORPORATIONS

SAMPLE OF ORGANIZATIONAL MINUTES TO BEGIN BUSINESS, AND ELECT DIRECTORS/TRUSTEES AND CHURCH OFFICERS

AFTER INCORPORATION

Minutes of the Meeting

MINUTES OF THE FIRST MEETING OF

THE BOARD OF DIRECTORS OF

_____

(insert corporation name here)

The first meeting of Directors was held at _____ on the ___ day of _____ 20_____ at _____ _.m.

The following were present: (names) being a quorum and all the Directors of the corporation.

(Name) called the meeting to order. Upon motion duly made, seconded, and carried, _____ was duly elected Chairperson of the meeting and _____ was duly elected Secretary thereof. They accepted their respective offices and proceeded with the discharge of their duties.

A written waiver of notice of this meeting signed by the Directors was submitted, read by the Secretary, and ordered appended to these minutes. The Secretary then presented and read to the meeting a certified copy of the certificate of incorporation of the corporation which was filed by Secretary of State of _____ on _____ 20___, and a copy of a determination letter from the Internal Revenue Service confirming the corporation's tax-exempt status under Section 501(C)(3) of the Internal Revenue Code. Upon motion duly made, seconded, and carried, these documents were accepted and the Secretary was directed to append them to these minutes for inclusion in the official records of the corporation.

The Chairperson stated that the election of officers was then in order.

The following were duly nominated, and, a vote having been taken, were unanimously elected officers of the corporation to serve for one year and until their successors are elected and qualified: (names.)

THE BEST GUIDE FOR NONPROFIT CORPORATIONS

SAMPLE OF WAIVER OF NOTICE

WAIVER OF NOTICE OF THE FIRST MEETING OF

THE BOARD OF DIRECTORS OF

_____

(insert corporation name here)

We, the undersigned, being all the Directors of the above corporation, hereby agree and consent that the first meeting of the board to be held on the date and at the time and place stated below for the purpose of electing officers and the transaction thereat of all such other business as may lawfully come before said meeting and hereby waive all notice of the meeting and of any adjournment thereof.

Place of meeting:_____
_____

Date of meeting: _____

Time of meeting:_____

_____
Director

_____
Director

_____
Director

Dated:_____, 20_____

THE BEST GUIDE FOR NONPROFIT CORPORATIONS

SAMPLE OF ORGANIZATIONAL MINUTES

ORGANIZATIONAL MINUTES OF THE SOLE DIRECTOR OF

_____
(insert corporation name here)

The undersigned, being the sole director of the corporation, organized under the General Corporation Law of _____ (state), took the following action to organize the corporation and in furtherance of its purposes and objectives on the date and at the place set forth below:

A certified copy of the certification of incorporation filed in the office of the Secretary of State on _____, 20____ and recorded in the office of the Recorder of the County of _____ on _____ , 20__ was appended to these minutes.

The office of the corporation was fixed at _____ in the City of _____ and State of _____.

Bylaws regulating the conduct of the affairs of the corporation were adopted and appended to these minutes for inclusion in the official records of the corporation.

The following were appointed officers of the corporation to serve for one year and until their successors are appointed or elected and qualified:

President: _____   Vice President: _____

Secretary: _____   Treasurer: _____

Each officer thereupon assumed the duties of his office.

There being no further business before the meeting, the same was adjourned.

Date: _____, 20_____

_____

President

THE BEST GUIDE FOR NONPROFIT CORPORATIONS

STEP 9 : SUBMIT YOUR INCORPORATING DOCUMENT

Mail your Articles of Incorporation to your state's office (the name and address of the state offices are listed in Chapter 6) or check the government pages of your phone book.) If you live near that office, you can hand carry your Articles of Incorporation and possibly get them approved the same day. Be sure to include a money order or cashier's check for the correct amount. Some states do not accept personal checks, so call to verify.

TIP: Make photocopies of everything you mail, even your money order or cashier's check. Some states require a cover letter sent in with the application. Also, if they ask that you send two (2) copies, make sure you send two copies.

STEP 10: YOU ARE OFFICIAL

If you didn't hand carry your application for incorporation to your state office, it will usually take about ten (10) working days to receive an approved copy. Once you receive it, you are in business. You can now file for an EIN (employer identification number) and apply for tax-exempt status, and receive donations.

TIP: You can solicit donations once you get your EIN. However, some businesses want to see your approved 501(C)(3) from the IRS. Don't let that discourage you. Ask for donations from the ones who will give you gifts based on your EIN. You don't have to mention that you don't have your 501(C)(3) unless they ask. If they do ask, be truthful and tell them that it's being processed.

CHAPTER SIX

Applying for Tax-Exempt Status

Applying for Tax-Exempt Status

This section is for charities, public foundation, and religious organizations under Section 501(C)(3) of the Internal Revenue Code. If you seek exemption under any other category, this will still help you through the process. The latest Application for Recognition of Exemption under Section 501(C)(3) of the Internal Revenue Code was prepared in September 1998. Since September 11, 2001, the application process is becoming a little tougher because the number of nonprofits increased tremendously. Don't be intimated by the name "IRS." The people who approved your application are people just like you and me. It is their job to help you, although some may not make it easy. So I will tell you this up front: It is not *unusual* for them to have more questions and return your application to you for clarification. Don't be discouraged. Call the number for the agent assigned to you and ask the agent to explain anything you don't understand. If the IRS has additional questions, they usually give you 30 days to respond by mail, (however, some will allow you to respond by fax).

The IRS gives one of two rulings to 501(C)(3) applicants, either a *definitive* or an *advance* ruling. Usually a church is issued a definitive ruling, which is a final and lasting ruling. An advance ruling is when the IRS will allow you to operate as a 501(C)(3) organization, but during the fifth year, they will ask if you would like continue, and based on the information provided, you may receive a definitive ruling. Usually, if you supply enough information, they will give you a definitive ruling the first time you apply.

*TIP: The IRS understands that new organizations usually have "dream applications," which means you may put the whole picture (vision) on paper but can't afford to operate like that. Be realistic. You can allow room for growth, but don't put on your application that you want to have 10 residential homes for the elderly or homeless when you're really starting with one (probably your own home.) Since you're not sure what your finances will be like, the IRS will likely give you an advance ruling so that you can be sure this is what you want to do. Five years from now, you may want to change the whole organization.*

If all your information establishes that your organization meets the requirements for exemption, the IRS will issue a determination letter recognizing your organization's exempt status and providing its public-charity classification. This is an important document that should be kept in the organization's permanent records.

AFTER BEING APPROVED FOR 501(C)(3) STATUS, IT'S IMPORTANT THAT YOU MAINTAIN RECORDS OF ALL TRANSACTIONS.

Record Keeping

There is no law that states how long you should keep records. Personally, as long as you are in business, I would keep certain records of financial activity. Section 501(C)(3) organizations are required to keep books and records detailing all activities, both financial and nonfinancial. Financial information, particularly information on its sources of support (contributions, grants, sponsorships, and other sources of revenue.) If you receive an advance ruling, good record keeping is crucial to determining an organization's private foundation status. Also, organizations must make their application (Form 1023) and the three most recent annual returns (Form 990 or Form 990-EZ) available to the public, upon request and without charge (except for a reasonable charge for copying.) The IRS also makes these documents available for public inspection and copying. These documents must be made available at the organization's principal office during regular business hours. Upon request, an organization must furnish copies of the application and the three most recent annual returns. The requests may be made in person or in writing.

Organizations that are tax exempt under section 501(C)(3) of the IRC must meet certain requirements for documenting charitable contributions. The federal tax law imposes two general disclosure rules: 1) a donor must obtain a written acknowledgment from a charity for any single contribution of $250 or more before the donor can claim a charitable contribution on his federal income tax return; 2) a charitable organization must provide a written disclosure to a donor who makes a payment in excess of $75 partly as a contribution and partly for goods and services provided by the organization.

Examples of Written Acknowledgments

> *"Thank you for your cash contribution of $300 that (organization's name) received on December 12, 2003. No goods or services were provided in exchange for your contribution."*

> *"Thank you for your cash contribution of $350 that (organization's name) received on May 6, 2003. In exchange for your contribution, we gave you a cookbook with an estimated fair market value of $60."*

> *"Thank you for your contribution of a used oak baby crib and matching dresser that (organization's name) received on March 15, 2003. No goods or services were provided in exchange for your contribution."*

The following is an example of a written acknowledgment where a charity accepts contributions in the name of one of its activities:

> *"Thank you for your contribution of $450 to (organization's name) made in the name of its Special Relief Fund program. No goods or services were provided in exchange for your contribution."*

Filing Requirements

As mention earlier, you will have to pay an annual fee to stay incorporated, but there will not be any annual fees from the IRS. However, there are certain forms that must be filed:

<u>Annual Information Returns</u>

Organizations recognized as tax-exempt under section 501(C)(3) of the IRC may be required to file an annual information return: Form 990, Form 990-EZ, or Form 990-PF along with Schedules A and B. Certain categories of organizations are excepted from filing Form 990 or Form 990-EZ, including churches and very small organizations.

Unrelated Business Income Tax

In addition to filing Form 990, 990-EZ, or 990-PF, an exempt organization must file Form 990-T if it has $1,000 or more of gross receipts from an unrelated trade or business during the year. The organization must make quarterly payments of estimated tax on unrelated business income if it expects its tax for the year to be $500 or more. The organization may use Form 990-W to help calculate the amount of estimated payments required. In general, the tax is imposed on income from a regularly conducted trade or business that does not further the organization's exempt purposes (other than by providing funds.)

Employer Identification Number

An employer identification number (EIN) is a business' number with the IRS. Every business and tax-exempt organization, including churches, is required to have an EIN, whether or not it has any employees. The organization's EIN goes on all forms and correspondence to the IRS.

Apply for an EIN by completing Form SS-4, *Application for Employer Identification Number*, by calling toll-free (800) 829-4933; or by submitting an online form at www.irs.gov.

Try not to become impatient waiting for your EIN. If you apply by fax or mail, and then call the IRS' toll-free number. They're two different IRS offices, which means there is a good chance the IRS will issue two different ID numbers for your business. If this happens, you must get the IRS to remove one of the two numbers from its records; otherwise, they will think you are operating two different businesses with the same name and will mail you two different filing forms each year.

If you do have two numbers for the same business, call the IRS at (800) 829-4933, explain the problem, and ask for the "entity fax number" for your regional IRS office. You must then fax then a brief note to that fax number. In your letter, explain the discrepancy and tell the IRS which of the two numbers you plan to use. Address to: BMF: Business Master File. Make sure the number you want the IRS to keep on file is the number you used to open your business bank account.

Instructions for Form SS-4
(Rev. September 2003)

**Department of the Treasury
Internal Revenue Service**

For use with Form SS-4 (Rev. December 2001)
Application for Employer Identification Number.
Section references are to the Internal Revenue Code unless otherwise noted.

General Instructions

Use these instructions to complete **Form SS-4,** Application for Employer Identification Number. Also see **Do I Need an EIN?** on page 2 of Form SS-4.

Purpose of Form

Use Form SS-4 to apply for an employer identification number (EIN). An EIN is a nine-digit number (for example, 12-3456789) assigned to sole proprietors, corporations, partnerships, estates, trusts, and other entities for tax filing and reporting purposes. The information you provide on this form will establish your business tax account.

*An EIN is for use in connection with your business activities only. Do **not** use your EIN in place of your social security number (SSN).*

Items To Note

Apply online. You can now apply for and receive an EIN online using the internet. See **How To Apply** below.

File only one Form SS-4. Generally, a sole proprietor should file only one Form SS-4 and needs only one EIN, regardless of the number of businesses operated as a sole proprietorship or trade names under which a business operates. However, if the proprietorship incorporates or enters into a partnership, a new EIN is required. Also, each corporation in an affiliated group must have its own EIN.

EIN applied for, but not received. If you do not have an EIN by the time a return is due, write "Applied For" and the date you applied in the space shown for the number. **Do not** show your SSN as an EIN on returns.

If you do not have an EIN by the time a tax deposit is due, send your payment to the Internal Revenue Service Center for your filing area as shown in the instructions for the form that you are filing. Make your check or money order payable to the "United States Treasury" and show your name (as shown on Form SS-4), address, type of tax, period covered, and date you applied for an EIN.

How To Apply

You can apply for an EIN online, by telephone, by fax, or by mail depending on how soon you need to use the EIN. Use only one method for each entity so you do not receive more than one EIN for an entity.

Online. You can receive your EIN by internet and use it immediately to file a return or make a payment. Go to the IRS website at **www.irs.gov/businesses** and click on **Employer ID Numbers** under **topics.**

Telephone. You can receive your EIN by telephone and use it immediately to file a return or make a payment. Call the IRS at **1-800-829-4933.** (International applicants must call 215-516-6999.) The hours of operation are 7:00 a.m. to 10:00 p.m. The person making the call must be authorized to sign the form or be an authorized designee. See **Signature** and **Third Party Designee** on page 6. Also see the **TIP** below.

If you are applying by telephone, it will be helpful to complete Form SS-4 before contacting the IRS. An IRS representative will use the information from the Form SS-4 to establish your account and assign you an EIN. Write the number you are given on the upper right corner of the form and sign and date it. Keep this copy for your records.

If requested by an IRS representative, mail or fax (facsimile) the signed Form SS-4 (including any Third Party Designee authorization) within 24 hours to the IRS address provided by the IRS representative.

*Taxpayer representatives can apply for an EIN on behalf of their client and request that the EIN be faxed to their **client** on the same day.*
Note: *By using this procedure, you are authorizing the IRS to fax the EIN without a cover sheet.*

Fax. Under the Fax-TIN program, you can receive your EIN by fax within 4 business days. Complete and fax Form SS-4 to the IRS using the Fax-TIN number listed on page 2 for your state. A long-distance charge to callers outside of the local calling area will apply. Fax-TIN numbers can only be used to apply for an EIN. **The numbers may change without notice.** Fax-TIN is available 24 hours a day, 7 days a week.

Be sure to provide your fax number so the IRS can fax the EIN back to you. **Note:** By using this procedure, you are authorizing the IRS to fax the EIN without a cover sheet.

Mail. Complete Form SS-4 at least 4 to 5 weeks before you will need an EIN. Sign and date the application and mail it to the service center address for your state. You will receive your EIN in the mail in approximately 4 weeks. See also **Third Party Designee** on page 6.

Call 1-800-829-4933 to verify a number or to ask about the status of an application by mail.

Cat. No. 62736F

Where To Fax or File

If your principal business, office or agency, or legal residence in the case of an individual, is located in:	Call the Fax-TIN number shown or file with the "Internal Revenue Service Center" at:
Connecticut, Delaware, District of Columbia, Florida, Georgia, Maine, Maryland, Massachusetts, New Hampshire, New Jersey, New York, North Carolina, Ohio, Pennsylvania, Rhode Island, South Carolina, Vermont, Virginia, West Virginia	Attn: EIN Operation P. O. Box 9003 Holtsville, NY 11742-9003 Fax-TIN 631-447-8960
Illinois, Indiana, Kentucky, Michigan	Attn: EIN Operation Cincinnati, OH 45999 Fax-TIN 859-669-5760
Alabama, Alaska, Arizona, Arkansas, California, Colorado, Hawaii, Idaho, Iowa, Kansas, Louisiana, Minnesota, Mississippi, Missouri, Montana, Nebraska, Nevada, New Mexico, North Dakota, Oklahoma, Oregon, Puerto Rico, South Dakota, Tennessee, Texas, Utah, Washington, Wisconsin, Wyoming	Attn: EIN Operation Philadelphia, PA 19255 Fax-TIN 215-516-3990
If you have no legal residence, principal place of business, or principal office or agency in any state:	Attn: EIN Operation Philadelphia, PA 19255 Telephone 215-516-6999 Fax-TIN 215-516-3990

How To Get Forms and Publications

Phone. You can order forms, instructions, and publications by phone 24 hours a day, 7 days a week. Call 1-800-TAX-FORM (1-800-829-3676). You should receive your order or notification of its status within 10 workdays.

Personal computer. With your personal computer and modem, you can get the forms and information you need using the IRS website at **www.irs.gov** or File Transfer Protocol at **ftp.irs.gov**.

CD-ROM. For small businesses, return preparers, or others who may frequently need tax forms or publications, a CD-ROM containing over 2,000 tax products (including many prior year forms) can be purchased from the National Technical Information Service (NTIS).

To order **Pub. 1796,** Federal Tax Products on CD-ROM, call **1-877-CDFORMS** (1-877-233-6767) toll free or connect to **www.irs.gov/cdorders**.

Tax Help for Your Business

IRS-sponsored Small Business Workshops provide information about your Federal and state tax obligations. For information about workshops in your area, call 1-800-829-4933.

Related Forms and Publications

The following **forms** and **instructions** may be useful to filers of Form SS-4:
- **Form 990-T,** Exempt Organization Business Income Tax Return
- **Instructions for Form 990-T**
- **Schedule C (Form 1040),** Profit or Loss From Business
- **Schedule F (Form 1040),** Profit or Loss From Farming
- **Instructions for Form 1041 and Schedules A, B, D, G, I, J, and K-1,** U.S. Income Tax Return for Estates and Trusts
- **Form 1042,** Annual Withholding Tax Return for U.S. Source Income of Foreign Persons
- **Instructions for Form 1065,** U.S. Return of Partnership Income
- **Instructions for Form 1066,** U.S. Real Estate Mortgage Investment Conduit (REMIC) Income Tax Return
- **Instructions for Forms 1120 and 1120-A**
- **Form 2553,** Election by a Small Business Corporation
- **Form 2848,** Power of Attorney and Declaration of Representative
- **Form 8821,** Tax Information Authorization
- **Form 8832,** Entity Classification Election

For more **information** about filing Form SS-4 and related issues, see:
- **Circular A,** Agricultural Employer's Tax Guide (Pub. 51)
- **Circular E,** Employer's Tax Guide (Pub. 15)
- **Pub. 538,** Accounting Periods and Methods
- **Pub. 542,** Corporations
- **Pub. 557,** Exempt Status for Your Organization
- **Pub. 583,** Starting a Business and Keeping Records
- **Pub. 966,** Electronic Choices for Paying ALL Your Federal Taxes
- **Pub. 1635,** Understanding Your EIN
- **Package 1023,** Application for Recognition of Exemption Under Section 501(c)(3) of the Internal Revenue Code
- **Package 1024,** Application for Recognition of Exemption Under Section 501(a)

Specific Instructions

Print or type all entries on Form SS-4. Follow the instructions for each line to expedite processing and to avoid unnecessary IRS requests for additional information. Enter "N/A" (nonapplicable) on the lines that do not apply.

Line 1—Legal name of entity (or individual) for whom the EIN is being requested. Enter the legal name of the entity (or individual) applying for the EIN exactly as it appears on the social security card, charter, or other applicable legal document.

Individuals. Enter your first name, middle initial, and last name. If you are a sole proprietor, enter your individual name, not your business name. Enter your business name on line 2. Do not use abbreviations or nicknames on line 1.

Trusts. Enter the name of the trust.

Estate of a decedent. Enter the name of the estate.

Partnerships. Enter the legal name of the partnership as it appears in the partnership agreement.

Corporations. Enter the corporate name as it appears in the corporation charter or other legal document creating it.

Plan administrators. Enter the name of the plan administrator. A plan administrator who already has an EIN should use that number.

Line 2—Trade name of business. Enter the trade name of the business if different from the legal name. The trade name is the "doing business as " (DBA) name.

*Use the full legal name shown on line 1 on all tax returns filed for the entity. (However, if you enter a trade name on line 2 and choose to use the trade name instead of the legal name, enter the trade name on **all returns** you file.) To prevent processing delays and errors, **always** use the legal name only (or the trade name only) on **all** tax returns.*

Line 3—Executor, trustee, "care of" name. Trusts enter the name of the trustee. Estates enter the name of the executor, administrator, or other fiduciary. If the entity applying has a designated person to receive tax information, enter that person's name as the "care of" person. Enter the individual's first name, middle initial, and last name.

Lines 4a-b—Mailing address. Enter the mailing address for the entity's correspondence. If line 3 is completed, enter the address for the executor, trustee or "care of" person. Generally, this address will be used on all tax returns.

*File **Form 8822**, Change of Address, to report any subsequent changes to the entity's mailing address.*

Lines 5a-b—Street address. Provide the entity's physical address **only** if different from its mailing address shown in lines 4a-b. **Do not** enter a P.O. box number here.

Line 6—County and state where principal business is located. Enter the entity's primary **physical** location.

Lines 7a-b—Name of principal officer, general partner, grantor, owner, or trustor. Enter the first name, middle initial, last name, and SSN of **(a)** the principal officer if the business is a corporation, **(b)** a general partner if a partnership, **(c)** the owner of an entity that is disregarded as separate from its owner (disregarded entities owned by a corporation enter the corporation's name and EIN), or **(d)** a grantor, owner, or trustor if a trust.

If the person in question is an **alien individual** with a previously assigned individual taxpayer identification number (ITIN), enter the ITIN in the space provided and submit a copy of an official identifying document. If necessary, complete **Form W-7,** Application for IRS Individual Taxpayer Identification Number, to obtain an ITIN.

You are **required** to enter an SSN, ITIN, or EIN unless the only reason you are applying for an EIN is to make an entity classification election (see Regulations sections 301.7701-1 through 301.7701-3) and you are a nonresident alien with no effectively connected income from sources within the United States.

Line 8a—Type of entity. Check the box that best describes the type of entity applying for the EIN. If you are an alien individual with an ITIN previously assigned to you, enter the ITIN in place of a requested SSN.

*This is not an election for a tax classification of an entity. See **Limited liability company (LLC)** on page 4.*

Other. If not specifically listed, check the "Other" box, enter the type of entity and the type of return, if any, that will be filed (for example, "Common Trust Fund, Form 1065" or "Created a Pension Plan"). Do not enter "N/A." If you are an alien individual applying for an EIN, see the **Lines 7a-b** instructions above.

• **Household employer.** If you are an individual, check the "Other" box and enter "Household Employer" and your SSN. If you are a state or local agency serving as a tax reporting agent for public assistance recipients who become household employers, check the "Other" box and enter "Household Employer Agent." If you are a trust that qualifies as a household employer, you do not need a separate EIN for reporting tax information relating to household employees; use the EIN of the trust.

• **QSub.** For a qualified subchapter S subsidiary (QSub) check the "Other" box and specify "QSub."

• **Withholding agent.** If you are a withholding agent required to file Form 1042, check the "Other" box and enter "Withholding Agent."

Sole proprietor. Check this box if you file Schedule C, C-EZ, or F (Form 1040) and have a qualified plan, or are required to file excise, employment, alcohol, tobacco, or firearms returns, or are a payer of gambling winnings. Enter your SSN (or ITIN) in the space provided. If you are a nonresident alien with no effectively connected income from sources within the United States, you do not need to enter an SSN or ITIN.

Corporation. This box is for any corporation **other than a personal service corporation.** If you check this box, enter the income tax form number to be filed by the entity in the space provided.

*If you entered **"1120S"** after the "Corporation" checkbox, the corporation **must** file Form 2553 **no later than the 15th day of the 3rd month of the tax year the election is to take effect.** Until Form 2553 has been received and approved, you will be considered a Form 1120 filer. See the Instructions for Form 2553.*

Personal service corp. Check this box if the entity is a personal service corporation. An entity is a personal service corporation for a tax year only if:

- The principal activity of the entity during the testing period (prior tax year) for the tax year is the performance of personal services substantially by employee-owners, and
- The employee-owners own at least 10% of the fair market value of the outstanding stock in the entity on the last day of the testing period.

Personal services include performance of services in such fields as health, law, accounting, or consulting. For more information about personal service corporations, see the Instructions for Forms 1120 and 1120-A and Pub. 542.

Other nonprofit organization. Check this box if the nonprofit organization is other than a church or church-controlled organization and specify the type of nonprofit organization (for example, an educational organization).

*If the organization also seeks tax-exempt status, you **must** file either Package 1023 or Package 1024. See Pub. 557 for more information.*

If the organization is covered by a group exemption letter, enter the four-digit **group exemption number (GEN).** (Do not confuse the GEN with the nine-digit EIN.) If you do not know the GEN, contact the parent organization. Get Pub. 557 for more information about group exemption numbers.

Plan administrator. If the plan administrator is an individual, enter the plan administrator's SSN in the space provided.

REMIC. Check this box if the entity has elected to be treated as a real estate mortgage investment conduit (REMIC). See the Instructions for Form 1066 for more information.

Limited liability company (LLC). An LLC is an entity organized under the laws of a state or foreign country as a limited liability company. For Federal tax purposes, an LLC may be treated as a partnership or corporation or be disregarded as an entity separate from its owner.

By **default,** a domestic LLC with only one member is **disregarded** as an entity separate from its owner and must include all of its income and expenses on the owner's tax return (e.g., **Schedule C (Form 1040)**). Also by default, a domestic LLC with two or more members is treated as a partnership. A domestic LLC may file Form 8832 to avoid either default classification and elect to be classified as an association taxable as a corporation. For more information on entity classifications (including the rules for foreign entities), see the instructions for Form 8832.

Do not** file Form 8832 if the LLC accepts the default classifications above. **However, if the LLC will be electing S Corporation status, it must timely file both Form 8832 and Form 2553.

Complete Form SS-4 for LLCs as follows:
- A single-member domestic LLC that accepts the default classification (above) does not need an EIN and generally should not file Form SS-4. Generally, the LLC should use the name and EIN of its **owner** for all Federal tax purposes. However, the reporting and payment of employment taxes for employees of the LLC may be made using the name and EIN of **either** the owner or the LLC as explained in Notice 99-6. You can find Notice 99-6 on page 12 of Internal Revenue Bulletin 1999-3 at **www.irs.gov/pub/irs-irbs/irb99-03.pdf.** (**Note:** If the LLC applicant indicates in box 13 that it has employees or expects to have employees, the owner (whether an individual or other entity) of a single-member domestic LLC will also be assigned its own EIN (if it does not already have one) even if the LLC will be filing the employment tax returns.)
- A single-member, domestic LLC that accepts the default classification (above) and wants an EIN for filing employment tax returns (see above) or non-Federal purposes, such as a state requirement, must check the "Other" box and write "Disregarded Entity" or, when applicable, "Disregarded Entity—Sole Proprietorship" in the space provided.
- A multi-member, domestic LLC that accepts the default classification (above) must check the "Partnership" box.
- A domestic LLC that will be filing Form 8832 to elect corporate status must check the "Corporation" box and write in "Single-Member" or "Multi-Member" immediately below the "form number" entry line.

Line 9—Reason for applying. Check only **one** box. Do not enter "N/A."

Started new business. Check this box if you are starting a new business that requires an EIN. If you check this box, enter the type of business being started. **Do not** apply if you already have an EIN and are only adding another place of business.

Hired employees. Check this box if the existing business is requesting an EIN because it has hired or is hiring employees and is therefore required to file employment tax returns. **Do not** apply if you already have an EIN and are only hiring employees. For information on employment taxes (e.g., for family members), see Circular E.

You may be required to make electronic deposits of all depository taxes (such as employment tax, excise tax, and corporate income tax) using the Electronic Federal Tax Payment System (EFTPS). See section 11, Depositing Taxes, of Circular E and Pub. 966.

Created a pension plan. Check this box if you have created a pension plan and need an EIN for reporting purposes. Also, enter the type of plan in the space provided.

Check this box if you are applying for a trust EIN when a new pension plan is established. In addition, check the "Other" box in line 8a and write "Created a Pension Plan" in the space provided.

Banking purpose. Check this box if you are requesting an EIN for banking purposes only, and enter the banking purpose (for example, a bowling league for depositing dues or an investment club for dividend and interest reporting).

Changed type of organization. Check this box if the business is changing its type of organization. For example, the business was a sole proprietorship and has been incorporated or has become a partnership. If you check this box, specify in the space provided (including available space immediately below) the type of change made. For example, "From Sole Proprietorship to Partnership."

Purchased going business. Check this box if you purchased an existing business. **Do not** use the former owner's EIN unless you became the "owner" of a corporation by acquiring its stock.

Created a trust. Check this box if you created a trust, and enter the type of trust created. For example, indicate if the trust is a nonexempt charitable trust or a split-interest trust.

Exception. Do **not** file this form for certain grantor-type trusts. The trustee does not need an EIN for the trust if the trustee furnishes the name and TIN of the grantor/owner and the address of the trust to all payors. See the Instructions for Form 1041 for more information.

Do not check this box if you are applying for a trust EIN when a new pension plan is established. Check "Created a pension plan."

Other. Check this box if you are requesting an EIN for any other reason; and enter the reason. For example, a newly-formed state government entity should enter "Newly-Formed State Government Entity" in the space provided.

Line 10—Date business started or acquired. If you are starting a new business, enter the starting date of the business. If the business you acquired is already operating, enter the date you acquired the business. If you are changing the form of ownership of your business, enter the date the new ownership entity began. Trusts should enter the date the trust was legally created. Estates should enter the date of death of the decedent whose name appears on line 1 or the date when the estate was legally funded.

Line 11—Closing month of accounting year. Enter the last month of your accounting year or tax year. An accounting or tax year is usually 12 consecutive months, either a calendar year or a fiscal year (including a period of 52 or 53 weeks). A calendar year is 12 consecutive months ending on December 31. A fiscal year is either 12 consecutive months ending on the last day of any month other than December or a 52-53 week year. For more information on accounting periods, see Pub. 538.

Individuals. Your tax year generally will be a calendar year.

Partnerships. Partnerships must adopt one of the following tax years:
- The tax year of the majority of its partners,
- The tax year common to all of its principal partners,
- The tax year that results in the least aggregate deferral of income, or
- In certain cases, some other tax year.

See the Instructions for Form 1065 for more information.

REMICs. REMICs must have a calendar year as their tax year.

Personal service corporations. A personal service corporation generally must adopt a calendar year unless:
- It can establish a business purpose for having a different tax year, or
- It elects under section 444 to have a tax year other than a calendar year.

Trusts. Generally, a trust must adopt a calendar year except for the following:
- Tax-exempt trusts,
- Charitable trusts, and
- Grantor-owned trusts.

Line 12—First date wages or annuities were paid or will be paid. If the business has or will have employees, enter the date on which the business began or will begin to pay wages. If the business does not plan to have employees, enter "N/A."

Withholding agent. Enter the date you began or will begin to pay income (including annuities) to a nonresident alien. This also applies to individuals who are required to file Form 1042 to report alimony paid to a nonresident alien.

Line 13—Highest number of employees expected in the next 12 months. Complete each box by entering the number (including zero ("-0-")) of "Agricultural," "Household," or "Other" employees expected by the applicant in the next 12 months. For a definition of agricultural labor (farmwork), see Circular A.

Lines 14 and 15. Check the **one** box in line 14 that best describes the principal activity of the applicant's business. Check the "Other" box (and specify the applicant's principal activity) if none of the listed boxes applies.

Use line 15 to describe the applicant's principal line of business in more detail. For example, if you checked the "Construction" box in line 14, enter additional detail such as "General contractor for residential buildings" in line 15.

Construction. Check this box if the applicant is engaged in erecting buildings or other structures, (e.g., streets, highways, bridges, tunnels). The term "Construction" also includes special trade contractors, (e.g., plumbing, HVAC, electrical, carpentry, concrete, excavation, etc. contractors).

Real estate. Check this box if the applicant is engaged in renting or leasing real estate to others; managing, selling, buying or renting real estate for others; or providing related real estate services (e.g., appraisal services).

Rental and leasing. Check this box if the applicant is engaged in providing tangible goods such as autos, computers, consumer goods, or industrial machinery and equipment to customers in return for a periodic rental or lease payment.

Manufacturing. Check this box if the applicant is engaged in the mechanical, physical, or chemical transformation of materials, substances, or components into new products. The assembling of component parts of manufactured products is also considered to be manufacturing.

Transportation & warehousing. Check this box if the applicant provides transportation of passengers or cargo; warehousing or storage of goods; scenic or sight-seeing transportation; or support activities related to these modes of transportation.

Finance & insurance. Check this box if the applicant is engaged in transactions involving the creation, liquidation, or change of ownership of financial assets and/or facilitating such financial transactions; underwriting annuities/insurance policies; facilitating such underwriting by selling insurance policies; or by providing other insurance or employee-benefit related services.

Health care and social assistance. Check this box if the applicant is engaged in providing physical, medical, or psychiatric care using licensed health care professionals or providing social assistance activities such as youth centers, adoption agencies, individual/family services, temporary shelters, etc.

Accommodation & food services. Check this box if the applicant is engaged in providing customers with lodging, meal preparation, snacks, or beverages for immediate consumption.

Wholesale–agent/broker. Check this box if the applicant is engaged in arranging for the purchase or sale of goods owned by others or purchasing goods on a commission basis for goods traded in the wholesale market, usually between businesses.

Wholesale–other. Check this box if the applicant is engaged in selling goods in the wholesale market generally to other businesses for resale on their own account.

Retail. Check this box if the applicant is engaged in selling merchandise to the general public from a fixed store; by direct, mail-order, or electronic sales; or by using vending machines.

Other. Check this box if the applicant is engaged in an activity not described above. Describe the applicant's principal business activity in the space provided.

Lines 16a-c. Check the applicable box in line 16a to indicate whether or not the entity (or individual) applying for an EIN was issued one previously. Complete lines 16b and 16c **only** if the "Yes" box in line 16a is checked. If the applicant previously applied for **more than one** EIN, write "See Attached" in the empty space in line 16a and attach a separate sheet providing the line 16b and 16c information for each EIN previously requested.

Third Party Designee. Complete this section **only** if you want to authorize the named individual to receive the entity's EIN and answer questions about the completion of Form SS-4. The designee's authority terminates at the time the EIN is assigned and released to the designee. **You must complete the signature area for the authorization to be valid.**

Signature. When required, the application must be signed by **(a)** the individual, if the applicant is an individual, **(b)** the president, vice president, or other principal officer, if the applicant is a corporation, **(c)** a responsible and duly authorized member or officer having knowledge of its affairs, if the applicant is a partnership, government entity, or other unincorporated organization, or **(d)** the fiduciary, if the applicant is a trust or an estate. Foreign applicants may have any duly-authorized person, (e.g., division manager), sign Form SS-4.

Privacy Act and Paperwork Reduction Act Notice. We ask for the information on this form to carry out the Internal Revenue laws of the United States. We need it to comply with section 6109 and the regulations thereunder which generally require the inclusion of an employer identification number (EIN) on certain returns, statements, or other documents filed with the Internal Revenue Service. If your entity is required to obtain an EIN, you are required to provide all of the information requested on this form. Information on this form may be used to determine which Federal tax returns you are required to file and to provide you with related forms and publications.

We disclose this form to the Social Security Administration for their use in determining compliance with applicable laws. We may give this information to the Department of Justice for use in civil and criminal litigation, and to the cities, states, and the District of Columbia for use in administering their tax laws. We may also disclose this information to Federal and state agencies to enforce Federal nontax criminal laws and to combat terrorism.

We will be unable to issue an EIN to you unless you provide all of the requested information which applies to your entity. Providing false information could subject you to penalties.

You are not required to provide the information requested on a form that is subject to the Paperwork Reduction Act unless the form displays a valid OMB control number. Books or records relating to a form or its instructions must be retained as long as their contents may become material in the administration of any Internal Revenue law. Generally, tax returns and return information are confidential, as required by section 6103.

The time needed to complete and file this form will vary depending on individual circumstances. The estimated average time is:

Recordkeeping	6 min.
Learning about the law or the form	22 min.
Preparing the form	46 min.
Copying, assembling, and sending the form to the IRS	20 min.

If you have comments concerning the accuracy of these time estimates or suggestions for making this form simpler, we would be happy to hear from you. You can write to the Tax Products Coordinating Committee, Western Area Distribution Center, Rancho Cordova, CA 95743-0001. **Do not** send the form to this address. Instead, see **How To Apply** on page 1.

Form SS-4
(Rev. December 2001)
Department of the Treasury
Internal Revenue Service

Application for Employer Identification Number

(For use by employers, corporations, partnerships, trusts, estates, churches, government agencies, Indian tribal entities, certain individuals, and others.)

▶ See separate instructions for each line.   ▶ Keep a copy for your records.

EIN

OMB No. 1545-0003

Type or print clearly.

1 Legal name of entity (or individual) for whom the EIN is being requested

2 Trade name of business (if different from name on line 1)

3 Executor, trustee, "care of" name

4a Mailing address (room, apt., suite no. and street, or P.O. box)

5a Street address (if different) (Do not enter a P.O. box.)

4b City, state, and ZIP code

5b City, state, and ZIP code

6 County and state where principal business is located

7a Name of principal officer, general partner, grantor, owner, or trustor

7b SSN, ITIN, or EIN

8a Type of entity (check only one box)
☐ Sole proprietor (SSN) _____
☐ Partnership
☐ Corporation (enter form number to be filed) ▶ _____
☐ Personal service corp.
☐ Church or church-controlled organization
☐ Other nonprofit organization (specify) ▶ _____
☐ Other (specify) ▶

☐ Estate (SSN of decedent) _____
☐ Plan administrator (SSN) _____
☐ Trust (SSN of grantor) _____
☐ National Guard   ☐ State/local government
☐ Farmers' cooperative   ☐ Federal government/military
☐ REMIC   ☐ Indian tribal governments/enterprises
Group Exemption Number (GEN) ▶ _____

8b If a corporation, name the state or foreign country (if applicable) where incorporated

State

Foreign country

9 Reason for applying (check only one box)
☐ Started new business (specify type) ▶ _____
☐ Hired employees (Check the box and see line 12.)
☐ Compliance with IRS withholding regulations
☐ Other (specify) ▶

☐ Banking purpose (specify purpose) ▶ _____
☐ Changed type of organization (specify new type) ▶ _____
☐ Purchased going business
☐ Created a trust (specify type) ▶ _____
☐ Created a pension plan (specify type) ▶ _____

10 Date business started or acquired (month, day, year)

11 Closing month of accounting year

12 First date wages or annuities were paid or will be paid (month, day, year). **Note:** *If applicant is a withholding agent, enter date income will first be paid to nonresident alien. (month, day, year)* . . . . ▶

13 Highest number of employees expected in the next 12 months. **Note:** *If the applicant does not expect to have any employees during the period, enter "-0-."* . . . . ▶

Agricultural	Household	Other

14 Check **one** box that best describes the principal activity of your business.   ☐ Health care & social assistance   ☐ Wholesale–agent/broker
☐ Construction   ☐ Rental & leasing   ☐ Transportation & warehousing   ☐ Accommodation & food service   ☐ Wholesale–other   ☐ Retail
☐ Real estate   ☐ Manufacturing   ☐ Finance & insurance   ☐ Other (specify)

15 Indicate principal line of merchandise sold; specific construction work done; products produced; or services provided.

16a Has the applicant ever applied for an employer identification number for this or any other business? . . . . ☐ Yes   ☐ No
Note: *If "Yes," please complete lines 16b and 16c.*

16b If you checked "Yes" on line 16a, give applicant's legal name and trade name shown on prior application if different from line 1 or 2 above.
Legal name ▶   Trade name ▶

16c Approximate date when, and city and state where, the application was filed. Enter previous employer identification number if known.
Approximate date when filed (mo., day, year)   City and state where filed   Previous EIN

Third Party Designee

Complete this section **only** if you want to authorize the named individual to receive the entity's EIN and answer questions about the completion of this form.

Designee's name

Designee's telephone number (include area code)
(   )

Address and ZIP code

Designee's fax number (include area code)
(   )

Under penalties of perjury, I declare that I have examined this application, and to the best of my knowledge and belief, it is true, correct, and complete.

Applicant's telephone number (include area code)
(   )

Name and title (type or print clearly) ▶

Applicant's fax number (include area code)
(   )

Signature ▶   Date ▶

For Privacy Act and Paperwork Reduction Act Notice, see separate instructions.   Cat. No. 16055N   Form **SS-4** (Rev. 12-2001)

Do I Need an EIN?

File Form SS-4 if the applicant entity does not already have an EIN but is required to show an EIN on any return, statement, or other document.[1] **See also the separate instructions for each line on Form SS-4.**

IF the applicant...	AND...	THEN...
Started a new business	Does not currently have (nor expect to have) employees	Complete lines 1, 2, 4a–6, 8a, and 9–16c.
Hired (or will hire) employees, including household employees	Does not already have an EIN	Complete lines 1, 2, 4a–6, 7a–b (if applicable), 8a, 8b (if applicable), and 9–16c.
Opened a bank account	Needs an EIN for banking purposes only	Complete lines 1–5b, 7a–b (if applicable), 8a, 9, and 16a–c.
Changed type of organization	Either the legal character of the organization or its ownership changed (e.g., you incorporate a sole proprietorship or form a partnership)[2]	Complete lines 1–16c (as applicable).
Purchased a going business[3]	Does not already have an EIN	Complete lines 1–16c (as applicable).
Created a trust	The trust is other than a grantor trust or an IRA trust[4]	Complete lines 1–16c (as applicable).
Created a pension plan as a plan administrator[5]	Needs an EIN for reporting purposes	Complete lines 1, 2, 4a–6, 8a, 9, and 16a–c.
Is a foreign person needing an EIN to comply with IRS withholding regulations	Needs an EIN to complete a Form W-8 (other than Form W-8ECI), avoid withholding on portfolio assets, or claim tax treaty benefits[6]	Complete lines 1–5b, 7a–b (SSN or ITIN optional), 8a–9, and 16a–c.
Is administering an estate	Needs an EIN to report estate income on Form 1041	Complete lines 1, 3, 4a–b, 8a, 9, and 16a–c.
Is a withholding agent for taxes on non-wage income paid to an alien (i.e., individual, corporation, or partnership, etc.)	Is an agent, broker, fiduciary, manager, tenant, or spouse who is required to file **Form 1042,** Annual Withholding Tax Return for U.S. Source Income of Foreign Persons	Complete lines 1, 2, 3 (if applicable), 4a–5b, 7a–b (if applicable), 8a, 9, and 16a–c.
Is a state or local agency	Serves as a tax reporting agent for public assistance recipients under Rev. Proc. 80-4, 1980-1 C.B. 581[7]	Complete lines 1, 2, 4a–5b, 8a, 9, and 16a–c.
Is a single-member LLC	Needs an EIN to file **Form 8832,** Classification Election, for filing employment tax returns, **or** for state reporting purposes[8]	Complete lines 1–16c (as applicable).
Is an S corporation	Needs an EIN to file **Form 2553,** Election by a Small Business Corporation[9]	Complete lines 1–16c (as applicable).

[1] For example, a sole proprietorship or self-employed farmer who establishes a qualified retirement plan, or is required to file excise, employment, alcohol, tobacco, or firearms returns, must have an EIN. **A partnership, corporation, REMIC (real estate mortgage investment conduit), nonprofit organization (church, club, etc.), or farmers' cooperative must use an EIN for any tax-related purpose even if the entity does not have employees.**

[2] However, **do not** apply for a new EIN if the existing entity only **(a)** changed its business name, **(b)** elected on Form 8832 to change the way it is taxed (or is covered by the default rules), or **(c)** terminated its partnership status because at least 50% of the total interests in partnership capital and profits were sold or exchanged within a 12-month period. (The EIN of the terminated partnership should continue to be used. See Regulations section 301.6109-1(d)(2)(iii).)

[3] Do not use the EIN of the prior business unless you became the "owner" of a corporation by acquiring its stock.

[4] However, IRA trusts that are required to file **Form 990-T,** Exempt Organization Business Income Tax Return, must have an EIN.

[5] A plan administrator is the person or group of persons specified as the administrator by the instrument under which the plan is operated.

[6] Entities applying to be a Qualified Intermediary (QI) need a QI-EIN even if they already have an EIN. **See Rev. Proc. 2000-12.**

[7] See also Household employer on page 4. (**Note:** State or local agencies may need an EIN for other reasons, e.g., hired employees.)

[8] Most LLCs **do not** need to file Form 8832. See **Limited liability company (LLC)** on page 4 for details on completing Form SS-4 for an LLC.

[9] An existing corporation that is electing or revoking S corporation status should use its previously-assigned EIN.

The Exemption Application

The IRS requires a payment of a one-time "user fee" with each application for a 501(C)(3) determination letter. For a new organization that anticipates gross receipts averaging not more than $10,000 during its first four years and (not more than $40,000 combined annual gross income for the first four years) the fee is *$150*

For a new organization that anticipates gross receipts averaging more than $10,000 during its first four years (more than $40,000.00 combined annual gross income for the first four years) the fee *$500*

The IRS cannot waive this user fee - it's mandated by Congress. The user fee will be refunded only if the IRS declines to issue a determination for reasons other than an organization's failure to supply requested information.

Complete Form 1023, *Application for Recognition of Exemption Under Section 501(C)(3) of the Internal Revenue Code*, and mail to the address indicated in the instructions. The required user fee must accompany Form 1023. The IRS will not process an application until the user fee is paid.

New organizations must give financial statements for the current year and proposed budgets for the next two years, including a detailed breakdown of revenue and expenses. Provide this information on Form 1023, Part IV. (In some cases, an organization filing Form 1023 must also file Form 872-C consenting to an extension of the statute under which the IRS can assess tax on net investment income for private foundations.)

You must also fill out and send *Form 8718, User Fee for Exempt Organization Determination Letter Request* along with the appropriate user fee in a check or money order made payable to the Internal Revenue Service. Mail these with your application for exemption (Form 1023.)

You must also fill out and attach Form 2848, *Power of Attorney and Declaration of Representative*, if someone other than your principal officer or director will represent you on matters regarding the application.

Fill out and attach Form 8821, *Tax Information Authorization*, if you want the IRS to provide information about your application to an employee other than a principal officer or director.

This is an example of what you would type on the exemption application (Form 1023, Part II):

One of the most complicated parts of completing the application for exemption is writing a description of your activities.

Activity	Date	By whom	% of time
1. To operate a 24 hour residential home to provide emotional support, motivation, and a greater degree of self-worth while addressing the mental & emotional needs of women.	7/04	Staff & Volunteers	30%
2. Develop a network of professional volunteer counselors who would volunteer to give free counseling to women & families.	4/04	Staff & Volunteers	20%
3. Fund-raising	5/04	Staff & Volunteers	30%
4. Supply needs of women by being a hub or network center for linking individuals in need to churches, nonprofit organizations, and corporations who could assist them with jobs, and health issues when necessary.	7/04	Staff & Volunteers	20%

What will be the sources of financial support?

    Public Support 60%

    Private Individuals 20%

    Grants 20%

Department of the Treasury
Internal Revenue Service

Application for Recognition of Exemption

Under Section 501(c)(3) of the Internal Revenue Code

Contents:
Form 1023 and
  Instructions
Form 872-C

Note: *For the addresses for filing **Form 1023**, see **Form 8718**, User Fee for Exempt Organization Determination Letter Request.*

*For obtaining an employer identification number (EIN), see **Form SS-4**, Application for Employer Identification Number.*

Package 1023
(Rev. September 1998)

Cat. No. 47194L

**Department of the Treasury
Internal Revenue Service**

Instructions for Form 1023

(Revised September 1998)

Application for Recognition of Exemption Under Section 501(c)(3) of the Internal Revenue Code

Note: *Retain a copy of the completed Form 1023 in the organization's permanent records. See **Public Inspection of Form 1023** regarding public inspection of approved applications.*

General Instructions

Section references are to the Internal Revenue Code unless otherwise noted.

User Fee.—Submit with the Form 1023 application for a determination letter, a **Form 8718,** User Fee for Exempt Organization Determination Letter Request, and the user fee called for in the Form 8718. You may obtain Form 8718, and additional forms and publications, through your local IRS office or by calling 1-800-829-3676 (1-800-TAX-FORM). User fees are subject to change on an annual basis. Therefore, be sure that you use the most current Form 8718.

Helpful information.—For additional information, see:
- **Pub. 557,** Tax-Exempt Status for Your Organization
- **Pub. 598,** Tax on Unrelated Business Income of Exempt Organizations
- **Pub. 578,** Tax Information for Private Foundations and Foundation Managers
- **Internet site,** www.irs.ustreas.gov/bus_info/eo/

Purpose of Form

1. Completed Form 1023 required for section 501(c)(3) exemption.—Unless it meets one of the exceptions in **2** below, any organization formed after October 9, 1969, must file a Form 1023 to qualify as a section 501(c)(3) organization.

The IRS determines if an organization is a private foundation from the information entered on a Form 1023.

2. Organizations not required to file Form 1023.—The following types of organizations may be considered tax-exempt under section 501(c)(3) even if they do not file Form 1023:

1. Churches,

2. Integrated auxiliaries of churches, and conventions or associations of churches, or

3. Any organization that:

(a) Is not a private foundation (as defined in section 509(a)), and

(b) Has gross receipts in each taxable year of normally not more than $5,000.

Even if the above organizations are not required to file Form 1023 to be tax-exempt, these organizations may choose to file Form 1023 in order to receive a determination letter that recognizes their section 501(c)(3) status.

Section 501(c)(3) status provides certain incidental benefits such as:
- Public recognition of tax-exempt status.
- Advance assurance to donors of deductibility of contributions.
- Exemption from certain state taxes.
- Exemption from certain Federal excise taxes.
- Nonprofit mailing privileges, etc.

3. Other organizations.—Section 501(e) and (f) cooperative service organizations, section 501(k) child care organizations, and section 501(n) charitable risk pools use Form 1023 to apply for a determination letter under section 501(c)(3).

4. Group exemption letter.—Generally, Form 1023 is not used to apply for a group exemption letter. See Pub. 557 for information on how to apply for a group exemption letter.

What To File

All applicants must complete pages 1 through 9 of Form 1023. These organizations must also complete the schedules or form indicated:

1. Churches . . . . Schedule A
2. Schools . . . . Schedule B
3. Hospitals and Medical Research . . . . . . Schedule C
4. Supporting Organizations (509(a)(3)) . . . Schedule D
5. Private Operating Foundations . . . . Schedule E
6. Homes for the Aged or Handicapped . . . Schedule F
7. Child Care . . . . Schedule G
8. Scholarship Benefits or Student Aid . . . . Schedule H
9. Organizations that have taken over or will take over a "for profit" institution . . . . Schedule I
10. Organizations requesting an advance ruling in Part III, Line 10 . . . . Form 872-C

Attachments.—For any attachments submitted with Form 1023.—
- Show the organization's name, address, and employer identification number (EIN).
- Identify the Part and line item number to which the attachment relates.
- Use 8½ x 11 inch paper for any attachments.
- Include any court decisions, rulings, opinions, etc., that will expedite processing of the application. Generally, attachments in the form of tape recordings are not acceptable unless accompanied by a transcript.

When To File

An organization formed after October 9, 1969, must file Form 1023 to be recognized as an organization described in section 501(c)(3). Generally, if an organization files its application within 15 months after the end of the month in which it was formed, and if the IRS approves the application, the effective date of the organization's section 501(c)(3) status will be the date it was organized.

Generally, if an organization does not file its application (Form 1023) within 15 months after the end of the month in which it was formed, it will not qualify for exempt status during the period before the date of its application. For exceptions and special rules, including automatic extensions in some cases, see Part III of Form 1023.

The date of receipt of the Form 1023 is the date of the U.S. postmark on the cover in which an exemption application is mailed or, if no postmark appears on the cover, the date the application is stamped as received by the IRS.

Private delivery services.—See the instructions for your income tax return for information on certain private delivery services designated by the IRS to meet the "timely mailing as timely filing/paying rule." The private delivery service can tell you how to get written proof of the mailing date.

Caution: *Private delivery services cannot deliver items to P.O. boxes. You must use the U. S. Postal Service to mail any item to an IRS P.O. box address. See the Form 8718 for the P.O. box address as well as the express mail or a delivery service address.*

Where To File

File the completed Form 1023 application, and all required information, with the IRS at the address shown in Form 8718.

The IRS will determine the organization's tax-exempt status and whether any annual returns must be filed.

Signature Requirements

An officer, a trustee who is authorized to sign, or another person authorized by a power of attorney, must sign the Form 1023 application. Attach a power of attorney to the application. You may use **Form 2848,** Power of Attorney and Declaration of Representative, for this purpose.

Deductibility of Contributions

Donors can take a charitable contribution deduction if their gift or bequest is made to a section 501(c)(3) organization.

The effective date of an organization's section 501(c)(3) status determines the date that contributions to it are deductible by donors. (See **When To File** on page 1.)

Contributions by U.S. residents to foreign organizations generally are not deductible. Tax treaties between the U.S. and certain foreign countries provide limited exceptions. Foreign organizations (other than those in Canada or Mexico) that claim eligibility to receive contributions deductible by U.S. residents must attach an English copy of the U.S. tax treaty that provides for such deductibility.

Appeal Procedures

The organization's application will be considered by the IRS which will either:

1. Issue a favorable determination letter;

2. Issue a proposed adverse determination letter denying the exempt status requested; or

3. Refer the case to the National Office.

If the IRS sends you a proposed adverse determination, it will advise you of your appeal rights at that time.

Language and Currency Requirements

Language requirements.—Prepare the Form 1023 and attachments in English. Provide an English translation if the organizational document or bylaws are in any other language.

You may be asked to provide English translations of foreign language publications that the organization produces or distributes and that are submitted with the application.

Financial requirements.—Report all financial information in U.S. dollars (specify the conversion rate used). Combine amounts from within and outside the United States and report the total for each item on the financial statements.

For example:

Gross Investment Income	
From U.S. sources	$4,000
From non-U.S. sources	1,000
Amount to report on income statement	$5,000

Annual Information Return

If an annual information return is due while the organization's application for recognition of exempt status is pending with the IRS (including any appeal of a proposed adverse determination), the organization should file at the following address:

Internal Revenue Service
Ogden Service Center
Ogden, Utah 84201-0027

- **Form 990,** Return of Organization Exempt From Income Tax, **or**
- **Form 990-EZ,** Short Form Return of Organization Exempt From Income Tax, **and,**
- **Schedule A (Form 990),** Organization Exempt Under Section 501(c)(3), **or**
- **Form 990-PF,** Return of Private Foundation, if the organization acknowledges it is a private foundation, **and**

Indicate that an application is pending.

If an organization has unrelated business income of more than $1,000, file **Form 990-T,** Exempt Organization Business Income Tax Return.

Public Inspection of Form 1023

Caution: *Note the discussion below for the potential effect of the Taxpayer Bill of Rights 2 (TBOR2) on these instructions.*

IRS responsibilities for public inspection.—If the organization's application for section 501(c)(3) status is approved, the following items will be open to public inspection in any District office and at the National Office of the IRS (section 6104):

1. The organization's application and any supporting documents.

2. Any letter or other document issued by the IRS with regard to the application.

Note that the following items are not available for public inspection:

1. Any information relating to a trade secret, patent, style of work, or apparatus that, if released, would adversely affect the organization, or

2. Any other information that would adversely affect the national defense.

IMPORTANT: Applicants must identify this information by clearly marking it, "NOT SUBJECT TO PUBLIC INSPECTION," and must attach a statement to explain why the organization asks that the information be withheld. If the IRS agrees, the information will be withheld.

Organization's responsibilities for public inspection.—The organization must make available a copy of its approved application and supporting documents, along with any document or letter issued by the IRS for public inspection.

These documents must be available during regular business hours at the organization's principal office and at each of its regional or district offices having at least three paid employees. See Notice 88-120, 1988-2 C.B. 454.

A penalty of $20 a day will be imposed on any person under a duty to comply with the public inspection requirements for each day a failure to comply continues.

Furnishing copies of documents under TBOR2.—The Taxpayer Bill of Rights 2 (TBOR2), enacted July 30, 1996, modified prospectively the section 6685 penalty and the rules for the public inspection of returns and exemption applications. An organization must furnish a copy of its Form 990, Form 990-EZ, or exemption application, and certain related documents, if a request is made in writing or in person.

For a request made in person, the organization must make an immediate response.

For a response to a written request, the organization must provide the requested copies within 30 days.

The organization must furnish copies of its Forms 990, or Forms 990-EZ, for any of its 3 most recent taxable years. No charge is to be made other than charging a reasonable fee for reproduction and actual postage costs.

An organization need not provide copies if:

1. The organization has made the requested documents widely available in a manner provided in Treasury regulations, or

2. The Secretary of the Treasury determined, upon application by the organization, that the organization was subject to a harassment campaign such that a waiver of the obligation to provide copies would be in the public interest.

Penalty for failure to allow public inspection or provide copies.—The section 6685 penalty for willful failure to allow public inspections or provide copies is increased from the present-law level of $1,000 to $5,000 by TBOR2.

Effective date of TBOR2.—These public inspection provisions governing tax-exempt organizations under TBOR2 generally apply to requests made no earlier than 60 days after the date on which the Treasury Department publishes the regulations required under the provisions. However, Congress, in the legislative history of TBOR2, indicated that organizations would comply voluntarily with the public inspection provisions prior to the issuance of such regulations.

Special Rule for Canadian Colleges and Universities

A Canadian college or university that received **Form T2051,** Notification of Registration, from Revenue Canada (Department of National Revenue, Taxation) and whose registration has not been revoked, does not need to complete all parts of Form 1023.

Such an organization must complete only Part I of Form 1023 and Schedule B (Schools, Colleges, and Universities). It must attach a copy of its **Form T2050,** Application for Registration, together with all the required attachments submitted to Revenue Canada. It must furnish an English translation if any attachments were prepared in French.

Other Canadian organizations.—Other Canadian organizations that seek a determination of section 501(c)(3) status must complete Form 1023 in the same manner as U.S. organizations.

Specific Instructions

The following instructions are keyed to the line items on the application form:

Part I. Identification of Applicant

Line 1. Full name and address of organization.—Enter the organization's name exactly as it appears in its creating document including amendments. Show the other name in parentheses, if the organization will be operating under another name.

For a foreign address, enter the information in the following order: city, province or state, and country. Follow the country's practice in placing the postal code in the address. **Do not** abbreviate the country name.

Line 2. Employer identification number (EIN).—All organizations must have an EIN. Enter the nine-digit EIN the IRS assigned to the organization. See **Form SS-4,** Application for Employer Identification Number, for information on how to obtain an EIN immediately by telephone, if the organization does not have an EIN. Enter, "applied for," if the organization has applied for an EIN number previously. Attach a statement giving the date of the application and the office where it was filed. **Do not** apply for an EIN more than once.

Line 3. Person to contact.—Enter the name and telephone number of the person to contact during business hours if more information is needed. The contact person should be an officer, director, or a person with power of attorney who is familiar with the organization's activities and is authorized to act on its behalf. Attach Form 2848 or other power of attorney.

Line 4. Month the annual accounting period ends.—Enter the month the organization's annual accounting period ends. The accounting period is usually the 12-month period that is the organization's tax year. The organization's first tax year depends on the accounting period chosen. The first tax year could be less than 12 months.

Line 5. Date formed.—Enter the date the organization became a legal entity. For a corporation, this is the date that the articles of incorporation were approved by the appropriate state official. For an unincorporated organization, it is the date its constitution or articles of association were adopted.

Line 6.—Indicate if the organization is one of the following:
- 501(e)   Cooperative hospital service organization
- 501(f)   Cooperative service organization of operating educational organization
- 501(k)   Organization providing child care
- 501(n)   Charitable risk pool

If none of the above applies, make no entry on line 6.

Line 7.—Indicate if the organization has ever filed a Form 1023 or **Form 1024,** Application for Recognition of Exemption Under Section 501(a), with the IRS.

Line 8.—If the organization for which this application is being filed is a private foundation, answer "N/A." If the organization is not required to file Form 990 (or Form 990-EZ) and is not a private foundation, answer "No" and attach an explanation. See the Instructions for Form 990 and Form 990-EZ for a discussion of organizations not required to file Form 990 (or Form 990-EZ). Otherwise, answer "Yes."

Line 9.—Indicate if the organization has ever filed Federal income tax returns as a taxable organization or filed returns as an exempt organization (e.g., Form 990, 990-EZ, 990-PF, or 990-T).

Line 10. Type of organization and organizational documents.—
Organizing instrument.—Submit a conformed copy of the organizing instrument. If the organization does not have an organizing instrument, it will not qualify for exempt status.

A conformed copy is one that agrees with the original and all amendments to it. The conformed copy may be:

- A photocopy of the original signed and dated organizing document, OR
- A copy of the organizing document that is unsigned but is sent with a written declaration, signed by an authorized individual, that states that the copy is a complete and accurate copy of the original signed and dated document.

Corporation.—In the case of a corporation, a copy of the articles of incorporation, approved and dated by an appropriate state official, is sufficient by itself.

If an unsigned copy of the articles of incorporation is submitted, it must be accompanied by the written declaration discussed above.

Signed, or unsigned, copies of the articles of incorporation must be accompanied by a declaration stating that the original copy of the articles was filed with, and approved by, the state. The date filed must be specified.

Unincorporated association.—In the case of an unincorporated association, the conformed copy of the constitution, articles of association, or other organizing document must indicate, in the document itself, or in a written declaration, that the organization was formed by the adoption of the document by two or more persons.

Bylaws.—If the organization has adopted bylaws, include a current copy. The bylaws do not need to be signed if they are submitted as an attachment to the Form 1023 application. The bylaws of an organization alone are not an organizing instrument. They are merely the internal rules and regulations of the organization.

Trust.—In the case of a trust, a copy of the signed and dated trust instrument must be furnished.

Dissolution clause.—For an organization to qualify for exempt status, its organizing instrument must contain a proper dissolution clause, or state law must provide for distribution of assets for one or more section 501(c)(3) purposes upon dissolution. If the organization is relying on state law, provide the citation for the law and briefly state the law's provisions in an attachment. Foreign organizations must provide the citation for the foreign statute and attach a copy of the statute along with an English language translation.

See Pub. 557 for a discussion of dissolution clauses under the heading, **Articles of Organization, Dedication and Distribution of Assets.** Examples of dissolution clauses are shown in the sample organizing instruments given in that publication.

Organizational purposes.—The organizing instrument must specify the organizational purposes of the organization. The purposes specified must be limited to one or more of those given in section 501(c)(3). See Pub. 557 for detailed instructions and for sample organizing instruments that satisfy the requirements of section 501(c)(3) and the related regulations.

Part II. Activities and Operational Information

Line 1.—It is important that you report all activities carried on by the organization to enable the IRS to make a proper determination of the organization's exempt status.

Line 2.—If it is anticipated that the organization's principal sources of support will increase or decrease substantially in relation to the organization's total support, attach a statement describing anticipated changes and explaining the basis for the expectation.

Line 3.—For purposes of providing the information requested on line 3, "fundraising activity" includes the solicitation of contributions and both functionally related activities and unrelated business activities. Include a description of the nature and magnitude of the activities.

Line 4a.—Furnish the mailing addresses of the organization's principal officers, directors, or trustees. Do not give the address of the organization.

Line 4b.—The annual compensation includes salary, bonus, and any other form of payment to the individual for services while employed by the organization.

Line 4c.—Public officials include anyone holding an elected position or anyone appointed to a position by an elected official.

Line 4d.—For purposes of this application, a "disqualified person" is any person who, if the applicant organization were a private foundation, is:

   1. A "substantial contributor" to the foundation (defined below);

   2. A foundation manager;

   3. An owner of more than 20% of the total combined voting power of a corporation that is a substantial contributor to the foundation;

   4. A "member of the family" of any person described in **1, 2,** or **3** above;

   5. A corporation, partnership, or trust in which persons described in **1, 2, 3,** or **4** above, hold more than 35% of the combined voting power, the profits interest, or the beneficial interests; and

   6. Any other private foundation that is effectively controlled by the same persons who control the first-mentioned private foundation or any other private foundation substantially all of whose contributions were made by the same contributors.

A substantial contributor is any person who gave a total of more than $5,000 to the organization, and those contributions are more than 2% of all the contributions and bequests received by the organization from the date it was created up to the end of the year the contributions by the substantial contributor were received. A creator of a trust is treated as a substantial contributor regardless of the amount contributed by that person or others.

See Pub. 578 for more information on "disqualified persons."

Line 5.—If your organization controls or is controlled by another exempt organization or a taxable organization, answer "Yes." "Control" means that:

   1. Fifty percent (50%) or more of the filing organization's officers, directors, trustees, or key employees are also officers, directors, trustees, or key employees of the second organization being tested for control;

   2. The filing organization appoints 50% or more of the officers, directors, trustees, or key employees of the second organization; or

   3. Fifty percent (50%) or more of the filing organization's officers, directors, trustees, or key employees are appointed by the second organization.

   Control exists if the 50% test is met by any one group of persons even if collectively the 50% test is not met. Examples of special relationships are common officers and the sharing of office space or employees.

Line 6.—If the organization conducts any financial transactions (either receiving or distributing cash or other assets), or nonfinancial activities with an exempt organization (other than a 501(c)(3) organization), or with a political organization, answer "Yes," and explain.

Line 7.—If the organization must report its income and expense activity to any other organization (tax-exempt or taxable entity), answer "Yes."

Line 8.—Examples of assets used to perform an exempt function are: land, building, equipment, and publications. Do not include cash or property producing investment income. If you have no assets used in performing the organization's exempt function, answer "N/A."

Line 10a.—If the organization is managed by another exempt organization, a taxable organization, or an individual, answer "Yes."

Line 10b.—If the organization leases property from anyone or leases any of its property to anyone, answer "Yes."

Line 11.—A membership organization for purposes of this question is an organization that is composed of individuals or organizations who:

   1. Share in the common goal for which the organization was created;

   2. Actively participate in achieving the organization's purposes; and

   3. Pay dues.

Line 12.—Examples of benefits, services, and products are: meals to homeless people, home for the aged, a museum open to the public, and a symphony orchestra giving public performances.

Note: *Organizations that provide low-income housing should see Rev. Proc. 96-32, 1996-1 C.B. 717, for a "safe harbor" and an alternative facts and circumstances test to be used in completing line 12.*

Line 13.—An organization is attempting to influence legislation if it contacts or urges the public to contact members of a legislative body, for the purpose of proposing, supporting, or opposing legislation, or if it advocates the adoption or rejection of legislation.

   If you answer "Yes," you may want to file **Form 5768,** Election/Revocation of Election by an Eligible Section 501(c)(3) Organization To Make Expenditures To Influence Legislation.

Line 14.—An organization is intervening in a political campaign if it promotes or opposes the candidacy or prospective candidacy of an individual for public office.

Part III. Technical Requirements

Line 1.—If you check "Yes," proceed to line 7. If you check "No," proceed to line 2.

Line 2a.—To qualify as an integrated auxiliary, an organization must not be a private foundation and must satisfy the affiliation and support tests of Regulations section 1.6033-2(h).

Line 3.—Relief from the 15-month filing requirement is granted automatically if the organization submits a completed Form 1023 within 12 months from the end of the 15-month period.

   To get this extension, an organization must add the following statement at the top of its application: "Filed Pursuant to Section 301.9100-2." No request for a letter ruling is required to obtain an automatic extension.

Line 4.—See Regulation sections 301.9100-1 and 301.9100-3 for information about a discretionary extension beyond the 27-month period. Under these regulations, the IRS will allow an organization a reasonable extension of time to file a Form 1023 if it submits evidence to establish that:

   (a) It acted reasonably and in good faith, and

   (b) Granting relief will not prejudice the interests of the government.

Showing reasonable action and good faith.—An organization acted reasonably and showed good faith if at least one of the following is true.

   1. The organization filed its application before the IRS discovered its failure to file.

   2. The organization failed to file because of intervening events beyond its control.

   3. The organization exercised reasonable diligence but was not aware of the filing requirement.

   To determine whether the organization exercised reasonable diligence, it is necessary to take into account the complexity of filing and the organization's experience in these matters.

   4. The organization reasonably relied upon the written advice of the IRS.

   5. The organization reasonably relied upon the advice of a qualified tax professional who failed to file or advise the organization to file Form 1023. An organization cannot rely on the advice of a qualified tax professional if it knows or should know that he or she is not competent to render advice on filing exemption applications or is not aware of all the relevant facts.

Not acting reasonably and in good faith.—An organization has not acted reasonably and in good faith if it chose not to file after being informed of the requirement to file and the consequences of failure to do so. Furthermore, an organization has not acted reasonably and in good faith if it used hindsight to request an extension of time to file. That is, if after the original deadline to file passes, specific facts have changed so that filing an application becomes advantageous to an organization, the IRS will not ordinarily grant an extension. To qualify for an extension in this situation, the organization must prove that its decision to file did not involve hindsight.

No prejudice to the interest of the government.—Prejudice to the interest of the government results if granting an extension of time to file to an organization results in a lower total tax liability for the years to which the filing applies than would have been the case if the organization had applied on time. Before granting an extension, the IRS may require the organization requesting it to submit a statement from an independent auditor certifying that no prejudice will result if the extension is granted.

Procedure for requesting extension.—To request a discretionary extension, an organization must submit the following with its Form 1023:

- A statement showing the date Form 1023 should have been filed and the date it was actually filed.

- An affidavit describing in detail the events that led to the failure to apply and to the discovery of that failure. If the organization relied on a qualified tax professional's advice, the affidavit must describe the engagement and responsibilities of the professional and the extent to which the organization relied on him or her.

- All documents relevant to the election application.

- A dated declaration, signed by an individual authorized to act for the organization, that includes the following statement: "Under penalties of perjury, I declare that I have examined this request, including accompanying documents, and, to the best of my knowledge and belief, the request contains all the relevant facts relating to the request, and such facts are true, correct, and complete."

- A detailed affidavit from individuals having knowledge or information about the events that led to the failure to make the application and to the discovery of that failure. These individuals include accountants or attorneys knowledgeable in tax matters who advised the organization concerning the application. Any affidavit from a tax professional must describe the engagement and responsibilities of the professional as well as the advice that the professional provided to the organization. The affidavit must also include the name, current address, and taxpayer identification number of the individual making the affidavit (the affiant). The affiant must also forward with the affidavit a dated and signed declaration that states: "Under penalties of perjury, I declare that I have examined this request, including accompanying documents, and, to the best of my knowledge and belief, the request contains all the relevant facts relating to the request, and such facts are true, correct, and complete."

   The reasons for late filing should be specific to your particular organization and situation. Regulation section 301.9100-3 (see above) lists the factors the IRS will consider in determining if good cause exists for granting a discretionary extension of time to file the application. To address these factors, your response for line 4 should provide the following information:

1. Whether the organization consulted an attorney or accountant knowledgeable in tax matters or communicated with a responsible IRS employee (before or after the organization was created) to ascertain the organization's Federal filing requirements and, if so, the names and occupations or titles of the persons contacted, the approximate dates, and the substance of the information obtained;

2. How and when the organization learned about the 15-month deadline for filing Form 1023;

3. Whether any significant intervening circumstances beyond the organization's control prevented it from submitting the application timely or within a reasonable period of time after it learned of the requirement to file the application within the 15-month period; and

4. Any other information that you believe may establish reasonable action and good faith and no prejudice to the interest of the government for not filing timely or otherwise justify granting the relief sought.

A request for relief under this section is treated as part of the request for the exemption determination letter and is covered by the user fee submitted with Form 8718.

Line 5.—If you answer "No," the organization may receive an adverse letter limiting the effective date of its exempt status to the date its application was received.

Line 6.—The organization may still be able to qualify for exemption under section 501(c)(4) for the period preceding the effective date of its exemption as a section 501(c)(3) organization. If the organization is qualified under section 501(c)(4) and page 1 of Form 1024 is filed as directed, the organization will not be liable for income tax returns as a taxable entity. Contributions to section 501(c)(4) organizations are generally not deductible by donors as charitable contributions.

Line 7.—Private foundations are subject to various requirements, restrictions, and excise taxes under Chapter 42 of the Code that do not apply to public charities. Also, contributions to private foundations may receive less favorable treatment than contributions to public charities. See Pub. 578. Therefore, it is usually to an organization's advantage to show that it qualifies as a public charity rather than as a private foundation if its activities or sources of support permit it to do so. Unless an organization meets one of the exceptions below, it is a private foundation. In general, an organization is **not** a private foundation if it is:

1. A church, school, hospital, or governmental unit;

2. A medical research organization operated in conjunction with a hospital;

3. An organization operated for the benefit of a college or university that is owned or operated by a governmental unit;

4. An organization that normally receives a substantial part of its support in the form of contributions from a governmental unit or from the general public as provided in section 170(b)(1)(A)(vi);

5. An organization that normally receives not more than one-third of its support from gross investment income and more than one-third of its support from contributions, membership fees, and gross receipts related to its exempt functions (subject to certain exceptions) as provided in section 509(a)(2);

6. An organization operated solely for the benefit of, and in connection with, one or more organizations described above (or for the benefit of one or more of the organizations described in section 501(c)(4), (5), or (6) of the Code and also described in **5** above), but not controlled by disqualified persons other than foundation managers, as provided in section 509(a)(3); or

7. An organization organized and operated to test for public safety as provided in section 509(a)(4).

Line 8.—Basis for private operating foundation status: (Complete this line **only** if you answered "Yes" to the question on line 7.)

A "private operating foundation" is a private foundation that spends substantially all of its adjusted net income or its minimum investment return, whichever is less, directly for the active conduct of the activities constituting the purpose or function for which it is organized and operated.

The foundation must satisfy the income test and one of the three supplemental tests: **(1)** the assets test; **(2)** the endowment test; or **(3)** the support test. For additional information, see Pub. 578.

Line 9.—Basis for nonprivate foundation status: Check the box that shows why your organization is not a private foundation.

Box (a). A church or convention or association of churches.

Box (b). A school.—See the definition in the instructions for Schedule B.

Box (c). A hospital or medical research organization.—See the instructions for Schedule C.

Box (d). A governmental unit.—This category includes a state, a possession of the United States, or a political subdivision of any of the foregoing, or the United States, or the District of Columbia.

Box (e). Organizations operated in connection with or solely for organizations described in (a) through (d) or (g), (h), and (i).—The organization must be organized and operated for the benefit of, to perform the functions of, or to carry out the purposes of one or more specified organizations described in section 509(a)(1) or (2). It must be operated, supervised, or controlled by or in connection with one or more of the organizations described in the instructions for boxes **(a)** through **(d)** or **(g), (h),** and **(i).** It must not be controlled directly or indirectly by disqualified persons (other than foundation managers or organizations described in section 509(a)(1) or (2)). To show whether the organization satisfies these tests, complete Schedule D.

Box (f). An organization testing for public safety.—An organization in this category is one that tests products to determine their acceptability for use by the general public. It does not include any organization testing for the benefit of a manufacturer as an operation or control in the manufacture of its product.

Box (g). Organization for the benefit of a college or university owned or operated by a governmental unit.—The organization must be organized and operated exclusively for the benefit of a college or university that:

• Is an educational organization within the meaning of section 170(b)(1)(A)(ii) and is an agency or instrumentality of a state or political subdivision of a state;

• Is owned or operated by a state or political subdivision of a state; OR

• Is owned or operated by an agency or instrumentality of one or more states or political subdivisions.

The organization must also normally receive a substantial part of its support from the United States or any state or political subdivision of a state, or from direct or indirect contributions from the general public or from a combination of these sources.

An organizaton described in section 170(b)(1)(A)(iv) will be subject to the same publicly supported rules that are applicable to 170(b)(1)(A)(vi) organizations described in box (h) below.

Box (h). Organization receiving support from a governmental unit or from the general public.—The organization must receive a substantial part of its support from the United States or any state or political subdivision, or from direct or indirect contributions from the general public, or from a combination of these sources.

The organization may satisfy the support requirement in either of two ways.

(1) It will be treated as publicly supported if the support it normally receives from the above-described governmental units and the general public equals at least one-third of its total support.

(2) It will also be treated as publicly supported if the support it normally receives from governmental or public sources equals at least 10% of total support and the organization is set up to attract new and additional public or governmental support on a continuous basis.

If the organization's governmental and public support is at least 10%, but not over one-third of its total support, the questions on lines 1 through 14 of Part II will apply to determine both the organization's claim of exemption and whether it is publicly supported. Preparers should exercise care to assure that those questions are answered in detail.

Box (i). Organization described in section 509(a)(2).—The organization must satisfy the support test under section 509(a)(2)(A) and the gross investment income test under section 509(a)(2)(B).

To satisfy the support test, the organization must normally receive more than one-third of its support from: **(a)** gifts, grants, contributions, or membership fees, and **(b)** gross receipts from admissions, sales of merchandise, performance of services, or furnishing of facilities, in an activity that is not an unrelated trade or business (subject to certain limitations discussed below).

This one-third of support must be from organizations described in section 509(a)(1), governmental sources, or persons other than disqualified persons.

In computing gross receipts from admissions, sales of merchandise, performance of services, or furnishing of facilities in an activity that is not an unrelated trade or business, the gross receipts from any one person or from any bureau or similar agency of a governmental unit are includible only to the extent they do not exceed the greater of $5,000 or 1% of the organization's total support.

To satisfy the gross investment income test, the organization must not receive more than one-third of its support from gross investment income.

Box (j).—If you believe the organization meets the public support test of section 170(b)(1)(A)(vi) or 509(a)(2) but are uncertain as to which public support test it satisfies, check box (j). By checking this box, you are claiming that the organization is not a private foundation and are agreeing to let the IRS compute the public support of your organization and determine the correct foundation status.

Line 10.—An organization must complete a tax year consisting of at least 8 months to receive a definitive (final) ruling under sections 170(b)(1)(A)(vi) and 509(a)(1), or under section 509(a)(2).

However, organizations that checked box **(h)**, **(i)**, or **(j)** on line 9 that do not meet the 8-month requirement must request an advance ruling that covers their first 5 tax years instead of requesting a definitive ruling.

An organization that meets the 8-month requirement has two options:

1. It may request a definitive ruling. The organization's public support computation will be based on the support the organization has received to date; or

2. It may request an advance ruling. The organization's public support computation will be based on the support it receives during its first 5 tax years.

An organization should consider the advance ruling option if it has not received significant public support during its first tax year or during its first and second tax years, but it reasonably expects to receive such support by the end of its fifth tax year.

An organization that receives an advance ruling is treated, during the 5-year advance ruling period, as a public charity (rather than a private foundation) for certain purposes, including those relating to the deductibility of contributions by the general public.

Line 11.—For definition of an unusual grant, see instructions for Part IV-A, line 12.

Line 12.—Answer this question only if you checked box **(g)**, **(h)**, or **(j)** on line 9.

Line 13.—Answer the question on this line only if you checked box **(i)** or **(j)** on line 9 and are requesting a definitive ruling on line 10.

Line 14.—Answer "Yes" or "No" on each line. If "Yes," you must complete the appropriate schedule. Each schedule is included in this application package with accompanying instructions. For a brief definition of each type of organization, see the appropriate schedule.

Part IV. Financial Data

Complete the Statement of Revenue and Expenses for the current year and each of the 3 years immediately before it (or the years the organization has existed, if less than 4).

Any applicant that has existed for less than 1 year must give financial data for the current year and proposed budgets for the following 2 years.

The IRS may request financial data for more than 4 years if necessary.

All financial information for the current year must cover the period beginning on the first day of the organization's established annual accounting period and ending on any day that is within 60 days of the date of this application.

If the date of this application is less than 60 days after the first day of the current accounting period, no financial information is required for the current year.

Financial information is required for the 3 preceding years regardless of the current year requirements. Please note that if no financial information is required for the current year, the preceding year's financial information can end on any day that is within 60 days of the date of this application.

Prepare the statements using the method of accounting and the accounting period (entered on line 4 of Part I) the organization uses in keeping its books and records. If the organization uses a method other than the cash receipts and disbursements method, attach a statement explaining the method used.

A. Statement of Revenue and Expenses

Line 1.—Do not include amounts received from the general public or a governmental unit for the exercise or performance of the organization's exempt function. However, include payments made by a governmental unit to enable the organization to provide a service to the general public.

Do not include unusual grants. See the explanation for unusual grants in Line 12 of this section.

Line 2.—Include amounts received from members for the purpose of providing support to the organization. These are considered as contributions. Do not include payments to purchase admissions, merchandise, services, or use of facilities.

Line 3.—Include on this line the income received from dividends, interest, and payments received on securities loans, rents, and royalties.

Line 4.—Enter the organization's net income from any activities that are regularly carried on and are not related to the organization's exempt purposes.

Examples of such income include fees from the commercial testing of products; income from renting office equipment or other personal property; and income from the sale of advertising in an exempt organization's periodical. See Pub. 598 for information about unrelated business income and activities.

Line 5.—Enter the amount collected by the local tax authority from the general public that has been allocated for your organization.

Line 6.—To report the value of services and/or facilities furnished by a governmental unit, use the fair market value at the time the service/facility was furnished to your organization. Do not include any other donated services or facilities in Part IV.

Line 7.—Enter the total income from all sources that is not reported on lines 1 through 6, or lines 9, 11, and 12. Attach a schedule that lists each type of revenue source and the amount derived from each.

Line 9.—Include income generated by the organization's exempt function activities (charitable, educational, etc.) and its nontaxable fundraising events (excluding any contributions received).

Examples of such income include the income derived by a symphony orchestra from the sale of tickets to its performances; and raffles, bingo, or other fundraising-event income that is not taxable as unrelated business income because the income-producing activities are not regularly carried on or because they are conducted with substantially all (at least 85%) volunteer labor. Record related cost of sales on line 22, Other.

Line 11.—Attach a schedule that shows a description of each asset, the name of the person to whom sold, and the amount received. In the case of publicly traded securities sold through a broker, the name of the purchaser is not required.

Line 12.—Unusual grants generally consist of substantial contributions and bequests from disinterested persons that:

1. Are attracted by reason of the publicly supported nature of the organization;

2. Are unusual and unexpected as to the amount; and

3. Would, by reason of their size, adversely affect the status of the organization as normally meeting the support test of section 170(b)(1)(A)(vi) or section 509(a)(2), as the case may be.

If the organization is awarded an unusual grant and the terms of the granting instrument provide that the organization will receive the funds over a period of years, the amount received by the organization each year under the grant may be excluded. See the regulations under sections 170 and 509.

Line 14.—Fundraising expenses represent the total expenses incurred in soliciting contributions, gifts, grants, etc.

Line 15.—Attach a schedule showing the name of the recipient, a brief description of the purposes or conditions of payment, and the amount paid. The following example shows the format and amount of detail required for this schedule:

Recipient	Purpose	Amount
Museum of Natural History	General operating budget	$29,000
State University	Books for needy students	14,500
Richard Roe	Educational scholarship	12,200

Colleges, universities, and other educational institutions and agencies subject to the Family Educational Rights and Privacy Act (20 U.S.C. 1232g) are not required to list the names of individuals who were provided scholarships or other financial assistance where such disclosure would violate the privacy provisions of the law. Instead, such organizations should group each type of financial aid provided, indicate the number of individuals who received the aid, and specify the aggregate dollar amount.

Line 16.—Attach a schedule showing the name of each recipient, a brief description of the purposes or condition of payment, and amount paid. Do not include any amounts that are on line 15. The schedule should be similar to the schedule shown in the line 15 instructions above.

Line 17.—Attach a schedule that shows the name of the person compensated; the office or position; the average amount of time devoted to the organization's affairs per week, month, etc.; and the amount of annual compensation. The following example shows the format and amount of detail required:

Name	Position	Time devoted	Annual salary
Philip Poe	President and general manager	16 hrs. per wk.	$27,500

Line 18.—Enter the total of employees' salaries not reported on line 17.

Line 19.—Enter the total interest expense for the year, excluding mortgage interest treated as if an occupancy expense on line 20.

Line 20.—Enter the amount paid for the use of office space or other facilities, heat, light, power, and other utilities, outside janitorial services, mortgage interest, real estate taxes, and similar expenses.

Line 21.—If your organization records depreciation, depletion, and similar expenses, enter the total.

Line 22.—Attach a schedule listing the type and amount of each **significant** expense for which a separate line is not provided. Report other miscellaneous expenses as a single total if not substantial in amount.

B. Balance Sheet

Line 1.—Enter the total cash in checking and savings accounts, temporary cash investments (money market funds, CDs, treasury bills, or other obligations that mature in less than 1 year), change funds, and petty cash funds.

Line 2.—Enter the total accounts receivable that arose from the sale of goods and/or performance of services, less any reserve for bad debt.

Line 3.—Enter the amount of materials, goods, and supplies purchased or manufactured by the organization and held to be sold or used in some future period.

Line 4.—Attach a schedule that shows the name of the borrower, a brief description of the obligation, the rate of return on the principal indebtedness, the due date, and the amount due. The following example shows the format and amount of detail required:

Name of borrower	Description of obligation	Rate of return	Due date	Amount
Hope Soap Corporation	Debenture bond (no senior issue outstanding)	8%	Jan. 2004	$37,500
Big Spool Company	Collateral note secured by company's fleet of 20 delivery trucks	10%	Jan. 2003	262,000

Line 5.—Attach a schedule listing the organization's corporate stock holdings.

For stock of closely held corporations, the statement should show the name of the corporation, a brief summary of the corporation's capital structure, and the number of shares held and their value as carried on the organization's books. If such valuation does not reflect current fair market value, also include fair market value.

For stock traded on an organized exchange or in substantial quantities over the counter, the statement should show the name of the corporation, a description of the stock and the principal exchange on which it is traded, the number of shares held, and their value as carried on the organization's books.

The following example shows the format and the amount of detail required:

Name of corporation	Capital structure (or exchange on which traded)	Shares	Book amount	Fair market value
Little Spool Corporation	100 shares nonvoting preferred issued and outstanding, no par value; 50 shares common issued and outstanding, no par value.			
	Preferred shares:	50	$20,000	$24,000
	Common shares:	10	25,000	30,000
Flintlock Corporation	Class A common N.Y.S.E.	80	6,000	6,500

Line 6.—Report each loan separately, even if more than one loan was made to the same person. Attach a schedule that shows the borrower's name, purpose of loan, repayment terms, interest rate, and original amount of loan.

Line 7.—Enter the book value of government securities held (U.S., state, or municipal). Also enter the book value of buildings and equipment held for investment purposes. Attach a schedule identifying and reporting the book value of each.

Line 8.—Enter the book value of buildings and equipment **not** held for investment. This includes plant and equipment used by the organization in conducting its exempt activities. Attach a schedule listing these assets held at the end of the current tax year/period and the cost or other basis.

Line 9.—Enter the book value of land **not** held for investment.

Line 10.—Enter the book value of each category of assets not reported on lines 1 through 9. Attach a schedule listing each.

Line 12.—Enter the total of accounts payable to suppliers and others, such as salaries payable, accrued payroll taxes, and interest payable.

Line 13.—Enter the unpaid portion of grants and contributions that the organization has made a commitment to pay to other organizations or individuals.

Line 14.—Enter the total of mortgages and other notes payable outstanding at the end of the current tax year/period. Attach a schedule that shows each item separately and the lender's name, purpose of loan, repayment terms, interest rate, and original amount.

Line 15.—Enter the amount of each liability not reported on lines 12 through 14. Attach a separate schedule.

Line 17.—Under fund accounting, an organization segregates its assets, liabilities, and net assets into separate funds according to restrictions on the use of certain assets. Each fund is like a separate entity in that it has a self-balancing set of accounts showing assets, liabilities, equity (fund balance), income, and expenses. If the organization does not use fund accounting, report only the "net assets" account balances, such as: capital stock, paid-in capital, and retained earnings or accumulated income.

Paperwork Reduction Act Notice.—We ask for the information on this form to carry out the Internal Revenue laws of the United States. If you want your organization to be recognized as tax-exempt by the IRS, you are required to give us this information. We need it to determine whether the organization meets the legal requirements for tax-exempt status.

The organization is not required to provide the information requested on a form that is subject to the Paperwork Reduction Act unless the form displays a valid OMB control number. Books or records relating to a form or its instructions must be retained as long as their contents may become material in the administration of any Internal Revenue law. The rules governing the confidentiality of the Form 1023 application are covered in Code section 6104.

The time needed to complete and file these forms will vary depending on individual circumstances. The estimated average times are:

Form	Recordkeeping	Learning about the law or the form	Preparing, and sending the form to IRS
1023 Parts I to IV	55 hr., 58 min.	5 hr., 1 min.	8 hr., 33 min.
1023 Sch. A	7 hr., 10 min.	-0- min.	7 min.
1023 Sch. B	4 hr., 47 min.	30 min.	36 min.
1023 Sch. C	5 hr., 1 min.	35 min.	43 min.
1023 Sch. D	4 hr., 4 min.	42 min.	47 min.
1023 Sch. E	9 hr., 20 min.	1 hr., 5 min.	1 hr., 17 min.
1023 Sch. F	2 hr., 39 min.	2 hr., 53 min.	3 hr., 3 min.
1023 Sch. G	2 hr., 38 min.	-0- min.	2 min.
1023 Sch. H	1 hr., 55 min.	42 min.	46 min.
1023 Sch. I	3 hr., 35 min.	-0- min.	4 min.
872-C	1 hr., 26 min.	24 min.	26 min.

If you have comments concerning the accuracy of these time estimates or suggestions for making these forms simpler, we would be happy to hear from you. You can write to the Tax Forms Committee, Western Area Distribution Center, Rancho Cordova, CA 95743-0001. **DO NOT** send the application to this address. Instead, see **Where To File** on page 1.

Procedural Checklist

Make sure the application is complete.

If you do not complete all applicable parts or do not provide all required attachments, we may return the incomplete application to your organization for resubmission with the missing information or attachments. This will delay the processing of the application and may delay the effective date of your organization's exempt status. The organization may also incur additional user fees.

Have you . . .

_____ Attached **Form 8718** (User Fee for Exempt Organization Determination Letter Request) and the appropriate fee?

_____ Prepared the application for mailing? (See **Where To File** addresses on Form 8718.) Do **not** file the application with your local Internal Revenue Service Center.

_____ Completed Parts I through IV and any other schedules that apply to the organization?

_____ Shown the organization's **Employer Identification Number (EIN)**?
  a. If your organization has an EIN, write it in the space provided.
  b. If this is a newly formed organization and does not have an Employer Identification Number, obtain an EIN by telephone. (See Specific Instructions, Part I, Line 2, on page 3.)

_____ Described your organization's **specific activities** as directed in Part II, line 1, of the application?

_____ Included a **conformed copy** of the complete organizing instrument? (See Specific Instructions, Part I, Line 10, on page 3.)

_____ Had the application signed by one of the following?
  a. An officer or trustee who is authorized to sign (e.g., president, treasurer); **or**
  b. A person authorized by a power of attorney (Submit Form 2848, or other power of attorney.)

_____ Enclosed **financial statements** (Part IV)?
  a. Current year (must include period up to within 60 days of the date the application is filed) and 3 preceding years.
  b. Detailed breakdown of revenue and expenses (no lump sums).
  c. If the organization has been in existence less than 1 year, you must also submit proposed budgets for 2 years showing the amounts and types of receipts and expenditures anticipated.

Note: *During the technical review of a completed application, it may be necessary to contact the organization for more specific or additional information.*

Do not send this checklist with the application.

Form **1023**
(Rev. September 1998)
Department of the Treasury
Internal Revenue Service

Application for Recognition of Exemption
Under Section 501(c)(3) of the Internal Revenue Code

OMB No. 1545-0056

Note: *If exempt status is approved, this application will be open for public inspection.*

Read the instructions for each Part carefully.
A User Fee must be attached to this application.
If the required information and appropriate documents are not submitted along with Form 8718 (with payment of the appropriate user fee), the application may be returned to you.
Complete the Procedural Checklist on page 8 of the instructions.

Part I — Identification of Applicant

1a Full name of organization (as shown in organizing document)

2 Employer identification number (EIN)
(If none, see page 3 of the **Specific Instructions**.)

1b c/o Name (if applicable)

3 Name and telephone number of person to be contacted if additional information is needed

1c Address (number and street) — Room/Suite

( )

1d City, town, or post office, state, and ZIP + 4. If you have a foreign address, see **Specific Instructions** for Part I, page 3.

4 Month the annual accounting period ends

5 Date incorporated or formed

1e Web site address

6 Check here if applying under section:
a ☐ 501(e) b ☐ 501(f) c ☐ 501(k) d ☐ 501(n)

7 Did the organization previously apply for recognition of exemption under this Code section or under any other section of the Code? . . . . ☐ Yes ☐ No
If "Yes," attach an explanation.

8 Is the organization required to file Form 990 (or Form 990-EZ)? . . . . ☐ N/A ☐ Yes ☐ No
If "No," attach an explanation (see page 3 of the **Specific Instructions**).

9 Has the organization filed Federal income tax returns or exempt organization information returns? . . ☐ Yes ☐ No
If "Yes," state the form numbers, years filed, and Internal Revenue office where filed.

10 Check the box for the type of organization. ATTACH A CONFORMED COPY OF THE CORRESPONDING ORGANIZING DOCUMENTS TO THE APPLICATION BEFORE MAILING. (See **Specific Instructions** for Part I, Line 10, on page 3.) See also Pub. 557 for examples of organizational documents.)

a ☐ **Corporation**—Attach a copy of the Articles of Incorporation (including amendments and restatements) showing approval by the appropriate state official; also include a copy of the bylaws.

b ☐ **Trust**— Attach a copy of the Trust Indenture or Agreement, including all appropriate signatures and dates.

c ☐ **Association**— Attach a copy of the Articles of Association, Constitution, or other creating document, with a declaration (see instructions) or other evidence the organization was formed by adoption of the document by more than one person; also include a copy of the bylaws.

If the organization is a corporation or an unincorporated association that has not yet adopted bylaws, check here ▶ ☐

I declare under the penalties of perjury that I am authorized to sign this application on behalf of the above organization and that I have examined this application, including the accompanying schedules and attachments, and to the best of my knowledge it is true, correct, and complete.

Please Sign Here ▶ _____ _____ _____
(Signature) (Type or print name and title or authority of signer) (Date)

For Paperwork Reduction Act Notice, see page 7 of the instructions.   Cat. No. 17133K

Form 1023 (Rev. 9-98) Page **2**

Part II Activities and Operational Information

1. Provide a detailed narrative description of all the activities of the organization—past, present, and planned. **Do not merely refer to or repeat the language in the organizational document.** List each activity separately in the order of importance based on the relative time and other resources devoted to the activity. Indicate the percentage of time for each activity. Each description should include, as a minimum, the following: **(a)** a detailed description of the activity including its purpose and how each acitivity furthers your exempt purpose; **(b)** when the activity was or will be initiated; and **(c)** where and by whom the activity will be conducted.

2. What are or will be the organization's sources of financial support? List in order of size.

3. Describe the organization's fundraising program, both actual and planned, and explain to what extent it has been put into effect. Include details of fundraising activities such as selective mailings, formation of fundraising committees, use of volunteers or professional fundraisers, etc. Attach representative copies of solicitations for financial support.

Form 1023 (Rev. 9-98) Page 3

Part II Activities and Operational Information (Continued)

4 Give the following information about the organization's governing body:

a Names, addresses, and titles of officers, directors, trustees, etc.	b Annual compensation

c Do any of the above persons serve as members of the governing body by reason of being public officials or being appointed by public officials? . . . . ☐ Yes ☐ No
If "Yes," name those persons and explain the basis of their selection or appointment.

d Are any members of the organization's governing body "disqualified persons" with respect to the organization (other than by reason of being a member of the governing body) or do any of the members have either a business or family relationship with "disqualified persons"? (See **Specific Instructions** for Part II, Line 4d, on page 3.) . . . . ☐ Yes ☐ No
If "Yes," explain.

5 Does the organization control or is it controlled by any other organization? . . . . ☐ Yes ☐ No
Is the organization the outgrowth of (or successor to) another organization, or does it have a special relationship with another organization by reason of interlocking directorates or other factors? . . . . ☐ Yes ☐ No
If either of these questions is answered "Yes," explain.

6 Does or will the organization directly or indirectly engage in any of the following transactions with any political organization or other exempt organization (other than a 501(c)(3) organization): **(a)** grants; **(b)** purchases or sales of assets; **(c)** rental of facilities or equipment; **(d)** loans or loan guarantees; **(e)** reimbursement arrangements; **(f)** performance of services, membership, or fundraising solicitations; or **(g)** sharing of facilities, equipment, mailing lists or other assets, or paid employees? . . . . . . ☐ Yes ☐ No
If "Yes," explain fully and identify the other organizations involved.

7 Is the organization financially accountable to any other organization? . . . . ☐ Yes ☐ No
If "Yes," explain and identify the other organization. Include details concerning accountability or attach copies of reports if any have been submitted.

Form 1023 (Rev. 9-98) Page **4**

Part II Activities and Operational Information *(Continued)*

8 What assets does the organization have that are used in the performance of its exempt function? (Do not include property producing investment income.) If any assets are not fully operational, explain their status, what additional steps remain to be completed, and when such final steps will be taken. If none, indicate "N/A."

9 Will the organization be the beneficiary of tax-exempt bond financing within the next 2 years? . . . . ☐ Yes ☐ No

10a Will any of the organization's facilities or operations be managed by another organization or individual under a contractual agreement? . . . . ☐ Yes ☐ No
  b Is the organization a party to any leases? . . . . ☐ Yes ☐ No
If either of these questions is answered "Yes," attach a copy of the contracts and explain the relationship between the applicant and the other parties.

11 Is the organization a membership organization? . . . . ☐ Yes ☐ No
If "Yes," complete the following:
  a Describe the organization's membership requirements and attach a schedule of membership fees and dues.

  b Describe the organization's present and proposed efforts to attract members and attach a copy of any descriptive literature or promotional material used for this purpose.

  c What benefits do (or will) the members receive in exchange for their payment of dues?

12a If the organization provides benefits, services, or products, are the recipients required, or will they be required, to pay for them? . . . . ☐ N/A ☐ Yes ☐ No
If "Yes," explain how the charges are determined and attach a copy of the current fee schedule.

  b Does or will the organization limit its benefits, services, or products to specific individuals or classes of individuals? . . . . ☐ N/A ☐ Yes ☐ No
If "Yes," explain how the recipients or beneficiaries are or will be selected.

13 Does or will the organization attempt to influence legislation? . . . . ☐ Yes ☐ No
If "Yes," explain. Also, give an estimate of the percentage of the organization's time and funds that it devotes or plans to devote to this activity.

14 Does or will the organization intervene in any way in political campaigns, including the publication or distribution of statements? . . . . ☐ Yes ☐ No
If "Yes," explain fully.

Form 1023 (Rev. 9-98) Page **5**

Part III Technical Requirements

1 Are you filing Form 1023 within 15 months from the end of the month in which your organization was created or formed? . . . . ☐ Yes ☐ No
If you answer "Yes," do not answer questions on lines 2 through 6 below.

2 If one of the exceptions to the 15-month filing requirement shown below applies, check the appropriate box and proceed to question 7.
Exceptions—You are not required to file an exemption application within 15 months if the organization:

☐ **a** Is a church, interchurch organization of local units of a church, a convention or association of churches, or an integrated auxiliary of a church. See **Specific Instructions,** Line 2a, on page 4;

☐ **b** Is not a private foundation and normally has gross receipts of not more than $5,000 in each tax year; or

☐ **c** Is a subordinate organization covered by a group exemption letter, but only if the parent or supervisory organization timely submitted a notice covering the subordinate.

3 If the organization does not meet any of the exceptions on line 2 above, are you filing Form 1023 within 27 months from the end of the month in which the organization was created or formed?. . . . . . ☐ Yes ☐ No

If "Yes," your organization qualifies under Regulation section 301.9100-2, for an automatic 12-month extension of the 15-month filing requirement. Do not answer questions 4 through 6.

If "No," answer question 4.

4 If you answer "No" to question 3, does the organization wish to request an extension of time to apply under the "reasonable action and good faith" and the "no prejudice to the interest of the government" requirements of Regulations section 301.9100-3? . . . . ☐ Yes ☐ No

If "Yes," give the reasons for not filing this application within the 27-month period described in question 3. See **Specific Instructions,** Part III, Line 4, before completing this item. Do not answer questions 5 and 6.

If "No," answer questions 5 and 6.

5 If you answer "No" to question 4, your organization's qualification as a section 501(c)(3) organization can be recognized only from the date this application is filed. Therefore, do you want us to consider the application as a request for recognition of exemption as a section 501(c)(3) organization from the date the application is received and not retroactively to the date the organization was created or formed? . ☐ Yes ☐ No

6 If you answer "Yes" to question 5 above and wish to request recognition of section 501(c)(4) status for the period beginning with the date the organization was formed and ending with the date the Form 1023 application was received (the effective date of the organization's section 501(c)(3) status), check here ▶ ☐ and attach a completed page 1 of Form 1024 to this application.

Form 1023 (Rev. 9-98) Page **6**

Part III Technical Requirements *(Continued)*

7 Is the organization a private foundation?
☐ **Yes** (Answer question 8.)
☐ **No** (Answer question 9 and proceed as instructed.)

8 If you answer "Yes" to question 7, does the organization claim to be a private operating foundation?
☐ **Yes** (Complete Schedule E.)
☐ **No**

After answering question 8 on this line, go to line 14 on page 7.

9 If you answer "No" to question 7, indicate the public charity classification the organization is requesting by checking the box below that most appropriately applies:

THE ORGANIZATION IS NOT A PRIVATE FOUNDATION BECAUSE IT QUALIFIES:

a	☐	As a church or a convention or association of churches (CHURCHES MUST COMPLETE SCHEDULE A.)	Sections 509(a)(1) and 170(b)(1)(A)(i)
b	☐	As a school (MUST COMPLETE SCHEDULE B.)	Sections 509(a)(1) and 170(b)(1)(A)(ii)
c	☐	As a hospital or a cooperative hospital service organization, or a medical research organization operated in conjunction with a hospital (These organizations, except for hospital service organizations, MUST COMPLETE SCHEDULE C.)	Sections 509(a)(1) and 170(b)(1)(A)(iii)
d	☐	As a governmental unit described in section 170(c)(1).	Sections 509(a)(1) and 170(b)(1)(A)(v)
e	☐	As being operated solely for the benefit of, or in connection with, one or more of the organizations described in **a** through **d, g, h,** or **i** (MUST COMPLETE SCHEDULE D.)	Section 509(a)(3)
f	☐	As being organized and operated exclusively for testing for public safety.	Section 509(a)(4)
g	☐	As being operated for the benefit of a college or university that is owned or operated by a governmental unit.	Sections 509(a)(1) and 170(b)(1)(A)(iv)
h	☐	As receiving a substantial part of its support in the form of contributions from publicly supported organizations, from a governmental unit, or from the general public.	Sections 509(a)(1) and 170(b)(1)(A)(vi)
i	☐	As normally receiving not more than one-third of its support from gross investment income and more than one-third of its support from contributions, membership fees, and gross receipts from activities related to its exempt functions (subject to certain exceptions).	Section 509(a)(2)
j	☐	The organization is a publicly supported organization but is not sure whether it meets the public support test of **h** or **i**. The organization would like the IRS to decide the proper classification.	Sections 509(a)(1) and 170(b)(1)(A)(vi) or Section 509(a)(2)

If you checked one of the boxes a through f in question 9, go to question 14. If you checked box g in question 9, go to questions 11 and 12. If you checked box h, i, or j, in question 9, go to question 10.

Form 1023 (Rev. 9-98) Page **7**

Part III Technical Requirements *(Continued)*

10 If you checked box **h, i,** or **j** in question 9, has the organization completed a tax year of at least 8 months?
☐ **Yes**—Indicate whether you are requesting:
  ☐ A definitive ruling. (Answer questions 11 through 14.)
  ☐ An advance ruling. (Answer questions 11 and 14 and attach two Forms 872-C completed and signed.)
☐ **No**—You must request an advance ruling by completing and signing two Forms 872-C and attaching them to the Form 1023.

11 If the organization received any unusual grants during any of the tax years shown in Part IV-A, **Statement of Revenue and Expenses,** attach a list for each year showing the name of the contributor; the date and the amount of the grant; and a brief description of the nature of the grant.

12 If you are requesting a definitive ruling under section 170(b)(1)(A)(iv) or (vi), check here ▶ ☐ and:

  a Enter 2% of line 8, column (e), Total, of Part IV-A . . . . _____
  b Attach a list showing the name and amount contributed by each person (other than a governmental unit or "publicly supported" organization) whose total gifts, grants, contributions, etc., were more than the amount entered on line **12a** above.

13 If you are requesting a definitive ruling under section 509(a)(2), check here ▶ ☐ and:
  a For each of the years included on lines 1, 2, and 9 of Part IV-A, attach a list showing the name of and amount received from each "disqualified person." (For a definition of "disqualified person," see **Specific Instructions,** Part II, Line 4d, on page 3.)
  b For each of the years included on line 9 of Part IV-A, attach a list showing the name of and amount received from each payer (other than a "disqualified person") whose payments to the organization were more than $5,000. For this purpose, "payer" includes, but is not limited to, any organization described in sections 170(b)(1)(A)(i) through (vi) and any governmental agency or bureau.

14	Indicate if your organization is one of the following. If so, complete the required schedule. (Submit only those schedules that apply to your organization. **Do not submit blank schedules.**)	Yes	No	If "Yes," complete Schedule:
	Is the organization a church?			A
	Is the organization, or any part of it, a school?			B
	Is the organization, or any part of it, a hospital or medical research organization?			C
	Is the organization a section 509(a)(3) supporting organization?			D
	Is the organization a private operating foundation?			E
	Is the organization, or any part of it, a home for the aged or handicapped?			F
	Is the organization, or any part of it, a child care organization?			G
	Does the organization provide or administer any scholarship benefits, student aid, etc.?			H
	Has the organization taken over, or will it take over, the facilities of a "for profit" institution? . . .			I

Form 1023 (Rev. 9-98) Page **8**

Part IV Financial Data

Complete the financial statements for the current year and for each of the 3 years immediately before it. If in existence less than 4 years, complete the statements for each year in existence. **If in existence less than 1 year, also provide proposed budgets for the 2 years following the current year.**

A. Statement of Revenue and Expenses

		Current tax year	3 prior tax years or proposed budget for 2 years				
		(a) From .... to	(b)	(c)	(d)	(e) TOTAL
Revenue	1 Gifts, grants, and contributions received (not including unusual grants—see page 6 of the instructions).						
	2 Membership fees received						
	3 Gross investment income (see instructions for definition)						
	4 Net income from organization's unrelated business activities not included on line 3.						
	5 Tax revenues levied for and either paid to or spent on behalf of the organization						
	6 Value of services or facilities furnished by a governmental unit to the organization without charge (not including the value of services or facilities generally furnished the public without charge).						
	7 Other income (not including gain or loss from sale of capital assets) (attach schedule)						
	8 **Total** (add lines 1 through 7)						
	9 Gross receipts from admissions, sales of merchandise or services, or furnishing of facilities in any activity that is not an unrelated business within the meaning of section 513. Include related cost of sales on line 22.						
	10 **Total** (add lines 8 and 9)						
	11 Gain or loss from sale of capital assets (attach schedule).						
	12 Unusual grants.						
	13 **Total** revenue (add lines 10 through 12).						
Expenses	14 Fundraising expenses						
	15 Contributions, gifts, grants, and similar amounts paid (attach schedule)						
	16 Disbursements to or for benefit of members (attach schedule).						
	17 Compensation of officers, directors, and trustees (attach schedule)						
	18 Other salaries and wages						
	19 Interest						
	20 Occupancy (rent, utilities, etc.).						
	21 Depreciation and depletion						
	22 Other (attach schedule)						
	23 **Total** expenses (add lines 14 through 22).						
	24 Excess of revenue over expenses (line 13 minus line 23)						

Form 1023 (Rev. 9-98) Page **9**

Part IV Financial Data (Continued)

B. Balance Sheet (at the end of the period shown)		Current tax year Date ....
Assets		
1 Cash	1	
2 Accounts receivable, net	2	
3 Inventories	3	
4 Bonds and notes receivable (attach schedule)	4	
5 Corporate stocks (attach schedule)	5	
6 Mortgage loans (attach schedule)	6	
7 Other investments (attach schedule)	7	
8 Depreciable and depletable assets (attach schedule)	8	
9 Land	9	
10 Other assets (attach schedule)	10	
11 **Total assets** (add lines 1 through 10)	11	
Liabilities		
12 Accounts payable	12	
13 Contributions, gifts, grants, etc., payable	13	
14 Mortgages and notes payable (attach schedule)	14	
15 Other liabilities (attach schedule)	15	
16 **Total liabilities** (add lines 12 through 15)	16	
Fund Balances or Net Assets		
17 Total fund balances or net assets	17	
18 **Total liabilities and fund balances or net assets** (add line 16 and line 17)	18	

If there has been any substantial change in any aspect of the organization's financial activities since the end of the period shown above, check the box and attach a detailed explanation . . . . ▶ ☐

Form **872-C**
(Rev. September 1998)

Department of the Treasury
Internal Revenue Service

Consent Fixing Period of Limitation Upon Assessment of Tax Under Section 4940 of the Internal Revenue Code

(See instructions on reverse side.)

OMB No. 1545-0056

To be used with Form 1023. Submit in duplicate.

Under section 6501(c)(4) of the Internal Revenue Code, and as part of a request filed with Form 1023 that the organization named below be treated as a publicly supported organization under section 170(b)(1)(A)(vi) or section 509(a)(2) during an advance ruling period,

----
(Exact legal name of organization as shown in organizing document)

(Number, street, city or town, state, and ZIP code)

and the District Director of Internal Revenue, or Assistant Commissioner (Employee Plans and Exempt Organizations)

consent and agree that the period for assessing tax (imposed under section 4940 of the Code) for any of the 5 tax years in the advance ruling period will extend 8 years, 4 months, and 15 days beyond the end of the first tax year.

However, if a notice of deficiency in tax for any of these years is sent to the organization before the period expires, the time for making an assessment will be further extended by the number of days the assessment is prohibited, plus 60 days.

Ending date of first tax year ----------------------------------
(Month, day, and year)

Name of organization (as shown in organizing document)	Date
Officer or trustee having authority to sign	Type or print name and title
Signature ▶	

For IRS use only

District Director or Assistant Commissioner (Employee Plans and Exempt Organizations)	Date
By ▶	

For Paperwork Reduction Act Notice, see page 7 of the Form 1023 Instructions.   Cat. No. 16905Q

Form 872-C (Rev. 9-98) Page **2**

You must complete Form 872-C and attach it to the Form 1023 if you checked box **h, i,** or **j** of Part III, question 9, and the organization has not completed a tax year of at least 8 months.

For example: If the organization incorporated May 15 and its year ends December 31, it has completed a tax year of only 7½ months. Therefore, Form 872-C must be submitted.

(a) Enter the name of the organization. This must be entered exactly as it appears in the organizing document. Do not use abbreviations unless the organizing document does.

(b) Enter the current address.

(c) Enter the ending date of the first tax year.

    For example:

        (1) If the organization was formed on June 15 and it has chosen December 31 as its year end, enter December 31, ...

        (2) If the organization was formed June 15 and it has chosen June 30 as its year end, enter June 30, ... In this example, the organization's first tax year consists of only 15 days.

(d) The form must be signed by an authorized officer or trustee, generally the president or treasurer. The name and title of the person signing must be typed or printed in the space provided.

(e) Enter the date that the form was signed.

DO NOT MAKE ANY OTHER ENTRIES.

Form 1023 (Rev. 9-98) Page **11**

Schedule A. Churches

1 Provide a brief history of the development of the organization, including the reasons for its formation.

---

2 Does the organization have a written creed or statement of faith? . . . . ☐ Yes ☐ No

If "Yes," attach a copy.

---

3 Does the organization require prospective members to renounce other religious beliefs or their membership in other churches or religious orders to become members? . . . . ☐ Yes ☐ No

---

4 Does the organization have a formal code of doctrine and discipline for its members? . . . . ☐ Yes ☐ No

If "Yes," describe.

5 Describe the form of worship and attach a schedule of worship services.

---

6 Are the services open to the public? . . . . ☐ Yes ☐ No

If "Yes," describe how the organization publicizes its services and explain the criteria for admittance.

---

7 Explain how the organization attracts new members.

---

8 **(a)** How many active members are currently enrolled in the church?

(b) What is the average attendance at the worship services?

---

9 In addition to worship services, what other religious services (such as baptisms, weddings, funerals, etc.) does the organization conduct?

Form 1023 (Rev. 9-98) Page **12**

Schedule A. Churches *(Continued)*

10 Does the organization have a school for the religious instruction of the young? . . . . ☐ **Yes** ☐ **No**

11 Were the current deacons, minister, and/or pastor formally ordained after a prescribed course of study? . . . . ☐ **Yes** ☐ **No**

12 Describe the organization's religious hierarchy or ecclesiastical government.

13 Does the organization have an established place of worship? . . . . ☐ **Yes** ☐ **No**

If "Yes," provide the name and address of the owner or lessor of the property and the address and a description of the facility.

If the organization has no regular place of worship, state where the services are held and how the site is selected.

14 Does (or will) the organization license or otherwise ordain ministers (or their equivalent) or issue church charters? . . . . ☐ **Yes** ☐ **No**

If "Yes," describe in detail the requirements and qualifications needed to be so licensed, ordained, or chartered.

15 Did the organization pay a fee for a church charter? . . . . ☐ **Yes** ☐ **No**

If "Yes," state the name and address of the organization to which the fee was paid, attach a copy of the charter, and describe the circumstances surrounding the chartering.

16 Show how many hours a week the minister/pastor and officers each devote to church work and the amount of compensation paid to each of them. If the minister or pastor is otherwise employed, indicate by whom employed, the nature of the employment, and the hours devoted to that employment.

Form 1023 (Rev. 9-98) Page **13**

Schedule A. Churches *(Continued)*

17 Will any funds or property of the organization be used by any officer, director, employee, minister, or pastor for his or her personal needs or convenience? ☐ **Yes** ☐ **No**

If "Yes," describe the nature and circumstances of such use.

18 List any officers, directors, or trustees related by blood or marriage.

19 Give the name of anyone who has assigned income to the organization or made substantial contributions of money or other property. Specify the amounts involved.

Instructions

Although a church, its integrated auxiliaries, or a convention or association of churches is not required to file Form 1023 to be exempt from Federal income tax or to receive tax-deductible contributions, such an organization may find it advantageous to obtain recognition of exemption. In this event, you should submit information showing that your organization is a church, synagogue, association or convention of churches, religious order or religious organization that is an integral part of a church, and that it is carrying out the functions of a church.

In determining whether an admittedly religious organization is also a church, the IRS does not accept any and every assertion that such an organization is a church. Because beliefs and practices vary so widely, there is no single definition of the word "church" for tax purposes. The IRS considers the facts and circumstances of each organization applying for church status.

The IRS maintains two basic guidelines in determining that an organization meets the religious purposes test:

 1. That the particular religious beliefs of the organization are truly and sincerely held, and

 2. That the practices and rituals associated with the organization's religious beliefs or creed are not illegal or contrary to clearly defined public policy.

In order for the IRS to properly evaluate your organization's activities and religious purposes, it is important that all questions in Schedule A be answered.

The information submitted with Schedule A will be a determining factor in granting the "church" status requested by your organization. In completing the schedule, consider the following points:

 1. The organization's activities in furtherance of its beliefs must be exclusively religious, and

 2. An organization will not qualify for exemption if it has a substantial nonexempt purpose of serving the private interests of its founder or the founder's family.

Schedule A. Churches *(Continued)*

Form 1023 (Rev. 9-98) Page **15**

Schedule B. Schools, Colleges, and Universities

1. Does, or will, the organization normally have: **(a)** a regularly scheduled curriculum, **(b)** a regular faculty of qualified teachers, **(c)** a regularly enrolled student body, and **(d)** facilities where its educational activities are regularly carried on? ☐ Yes ☐ No
If "No," do not complete the rest of Schedule B.

2. Is the organization an instrumentality of a state or political subdivision of a state? ☐ Yes ☐ No
If "Yes," document this in Part II and do not complete items 3 through 10 of Schedule B. (See instructions on the back of Schedule B.)

3. Does or will the organization (or any department or division within it) discriminate in any way on the basis of race with respect to:
    a. Admissions? ☐ Yes ☐ No
    b. Use of facilities or exercise of student privileges? ☐ Yes ☐ No
    c. Faculty or administrative staff? ☐ Yes ☐ No
    d. Scholarship or loan programs? ☐ Yes ☐ No
If "Yes" for any of the above, explain.

4. Does the organization include a statement in its charter, bylaws, or other governing instrument, or in a resolution of its governing body, that it has a racially nondiscriminatory policy as to students? ☐ Yes ☐ No

    Attach whatever corporate resolutions or other official statements the organization has made on this subject.

5. a. Has the organization made its racially nondiscriminatory policies known in a manner that brings the policies to the attention of all segments of the general community that it serves? ☐ Yes ☐ No

    If "Yes," describe how these policies have been publicized and how often relevant notices or announcements have been made. If no newspaper or broadcast media notices have been used, explain.

    b. If applicable, attach clippings of any relevant newspaper notices or advertising, or copies of tapes or scripts used for media broadcasts. Also attach copies of brochures and catalogs dealing with student admissions, programs, and scholarships, as well as representative copies of all written advertising used as a means of informing prospective students of the organization's programs.

6. Attach a numerical schedule showing the racial composition, as of the current academic year, and projected to the extent feasible for the next academic year, of: **(a)** the student body, and **(b)** the faculty and administrative staff.

7. Attach a list showing the amount of any scholarship and loan funds awarded to students enrolled and the racial composition of the students who have received the awards.

8. a. Attach a list of the organization's incorporators, founders, board members, and donors of land or buildings, whether individuals or organizations.

    b. State whether any of the organizations listed in **8a** have as an objective the maintenance of segregated public or private school education, and, if so, whether any of the individuals listed in **8a** are officers or active members of such organizations.

9. a. Enter the public school district and county in which the organization is located.

    b. Was the organization formed or substantially expanded at the time of public school desegregation in the above district or county? ☐ Yes ☐ No

10. Has the organization ever been determined by a state or Federal administrative agency or judicial body to be racially discriminatory? ☐ Yes ☐ No

    If "Yes," attach a detailed explanation identifying the parties to the suit, the forum in which the case was heard, the cause of action, the holding in the case, and the citations (if any) for the case. Also describe in detail what changes in the organization's operation, if any, have occurred since then.

For more information, see back of Schedule B.

Instructions

A "school" is an organization that has the primary function of presenting formal instruction, normally maintains a regular faculty and curriculum, normally has a regularly enrolled student body, and has a place where its educational activities are carried on.

The term generally corresponds to the definition of an "educational organization" in section 170(b)(1)(A)(ii). Thus, the term includes primary, secondary, preparatory and high schools, and colleges and universities. The term does not include organizations engaged in both educational and noneducational activities unless the latter are merely incidental to the educational activities. A school for handicapped children is included within the term, but an organization merely providing handicapped children with custodial care is not.

For purposes of Schedule B, "Sunday schools" that are conducted by a church are not included in the term "schools," but separately organized schools (such as parochial schools, universities, and similar institutions) are included in the term.

A private school that otherwise meets the requirements of section 501(c)(3) as an educational institution will not qualify for exemption under section 501(a) unless it has a racially nondiscriminatory policy as to students.

This policy means that the school admits students of any race to all the rights, privileges, programs, and activities generally accorded or made available to students at that school and that the school does not discriminate on the basis of race in the administration of its educational policies, admissions policies, scholarship and loan programs, and athletic or other school-administered programs.

The IRS considers discrimination on the basis of race to include discrimination on the basis of color and national or ethnic origin. A policy of a school that favors racial minority groups in admissions, facilities, programs, and financial assistance will not constitute discrimination on the basis of race when the purpose and effect is to promote the establishment and maintenance of that school's racially nondiscriminatory policy as to students.

See Rev. Proc. 75-50, 1975-2 C.B. 587, for guidelines and recordkeeping requirements for determining whether private schools that are applying for recognition of exemption have racially nondiscriminatory policies as to students.

Line 2

An instrumentality of a state or political subdivision of a state may qualify under section 501(c)(3) if it is organized as a separate entity from the governmental unit that created it and if it otherwise meets the organizational and operational tests of section 501(c)(3). See Rev. Rul. 60-384, 1960-2 C.B. 172. Any such organization that is a school is not a private school and, therefore, is not subject to the provisions of Rev. Proc. 75-50.

Schools that incorrectly answer "Yes" to line 2 will be contacted to furnish the information called for by lines 3 through 10 in order to establish that they meet the requirements for exemption. To prevent delay in the processing of your application, be sure to answer line 2 correctly and complete lines 3 through 10, if applicable.

Form 1023 (Rev. 9-98) Page **17**

Schedule C. Hospitals and Medical Research Organizations

☐ Check here if claiming to be a hospital; complete the questions in Section I of this schedule; and write "N/A" in Section II.
☐ Check here if claiming to be a medical research organization operated in conjunction with a hospital; complete the questions in Section II of this schedule; and write "N/A" in Section I.

Section I — Hospitals

1a How many doctors are on the hospital's courtesy staff? _____

b Are all the doctors in the community eligible for staff privileges? ☐ Yes ☐ No
If "No," give the reasons why and explain how the courtesy staff is selected.

2a Does the hospital maintain a full-time emergency room? ☐ Yes ☐ No

b What is the hospital's policy on administering emergency services to persons without apparent means to pay?

c Does the hospital have any arrangements with police, fire, and voluntary ambulance services for the delivery or admission of emergency cases? ☐ Yes ☐ No
Explain.

3a Does or will the hospital require a deposit from persons covered by Medicare or Medicaid in its admission practices? ☐ Yes ☐ No
If "Yes," explain.

b Does the same deposit requirement, if any, apply to all other patients? ☐ Yes ☐ No
If "No," explain.

4 Does or will the hospital provide for a portion of its services and facilities to be used for charity patients? ☐ Yes ☐ No
Explain the policy regarding charity cases. Include data on the hospital's past experience in admitting charity patients and arrangements it may have with municipal or government agencies for absorbing the cost of such care.

5 Does or will the hospital carry on a formal program of medical training and research? ☐ Yes ☐ No
If "Yes," describe.

6 Does the hospital provide office space to physicians carrying on a medical practice? ☐ Yes ☐ No
If "Yes," attach a list setting forth the name of each physician, the amount of space provided, the annual rent, the expiration date of the current lease and whether the terms of the lease represent fair market value.

Section II — Medical Research Organizations

1 Name the hospitals with which the organization has a relationship and describe the relationship.

2 Attach a schedule describing the organization's present and proposed (indicate which) medical research activities; show the nature of the activities, and the amount of money that has been or will be spent in carrying them out. (Making grants to other organizations is not direct conduct of medical research.)

3 Attach a statement of assets showing their fair market value and the portion of the assets directly devoted to medical research.

For more information, see back of Schedule C.

Additional Information

Hospitals

To be entitled to status as a "hospital," an organization must have, as its principal purpose or function, the providing of medical or hospital care or medical education or research. "Medical care" includes the treatment of any physical or mental disability or condition, the cost of which may be taken as a deduction under section 213, whether the treatment is performed on an inpatient or outpatient basis. Thus, a rehabilitation institution, outpatient clinic, or community mental health or drug treatment center may be a hospital if its principal function is providing the above-described services.

On the other hand, a convalescent home or a home for children or the aged is not a hospital. Similarly, an institution whose principal purpose or function is to train handicapped individuals to pursue some vocation is not a hospital. Moreover, a medical education or medical research institution is not a hospital, unless it is also actively engaged in providing medical or hospital care to patients on its premises or in its facilities on an inpatient or outpatient basis.

Cooperative Hospital Service Organizations

Cooperative hospital service organizations (section 501(e)) should not complete Schedule C.

Medical Research Organizations

To qualify as a medical research organization, the principal function of the organization must be the direct, continuous, and active conduct of medical research in conjunction with a hospital that is described in section 501(c)(3), a Federal hospital, or an instrumentality of a governmental unit referred to in section 170(c)(1).

For purposes of section 170(b)(1)(A)(iii) only, the organization must be set up to use the funds it receives in the active conduct of medical research by January 1 of the fifth calendar year after receipt. The arrangement it has with donors to assure use of the funds within the 5-year period must be legally enforceable.

As used here, "medical research" means investigations, experiments, and studies to discover, develop, or verify knowledge relating to the causes, diagnosis, treatment, prevention, or control of human physical or mental diseases and impairments.

For further information, see Regulations section 1.170A-9(c)(2).

Form 1023 (Rev. 9-98) Page **19**

Schedule D. Section 509(a)(3) Supporting Organizations

1a Organizations supported by the applicant organization:
Name and address of supported organization

b Has the supported organization received a ruling or determination letter that it is not a private foundation by reason of section 509(a)(1) or (2)?

Name and address of supported organization	Yes	No
	☐ Yes	☐ No
	☐ Yes	☐ No
	☐ Yes	☐ No
	☐ Yes	☐ No
	☐ Yes	☐ No

c If "No" for any of the organizations listed in **1a,** explain.

2 Does the supported organization have tax-exempt status under section 501(c)(4), 501(c)(5), or 501(c)(6)? ☐ Yes ☐ No
If "Yes," attach: **(a)** a copy of its ruling or determination letter, and **(b)** an analysis of its revenue for the current year and the preceding 3 years. (Provide the financial data using the formats in Part IV-A (lines 1–13) and Part III (lines 11, 12, and 13).)

3 Does your organization's governing document indicate that the majority of its governing board is elected or appointed by the supported organizations? . . . . ☐ Yes ☐ No
If "Yes," skip to line 9.
If "No," you must answer the questions on lines 4 through 9.

4 Does your organization's governing document indicate the common supervision or control that it and the supported organizations share? . . . . ☐ Yes ☐ No
If "Yes," give the article and paragraph numbers. If "No," explain.

5 To what extent do the supported organizations have a significant voice in your organization's investment policies, in the making and timing of grants, and in otherwise directing the use of your organization's income or assets?

6 Does the mentioning of the supported organizations in your organization's governing instrument make it a trust that the supported organizations can enforce under state law and compel to make an accounting? ☐ Yes ☐ No
If "Yes," explain.

7a What percentage of your organization's income does it pay to each supported organization?

b What is the total annual income of each supported organization?

c How much does your organization contribute annually to each supported organization?

For more information, see back of Schedule D.

Schedule D. Section 509(a)(3) Supporting Organizations *(Continued)*

8 To what extent does your organization conduct activities that would otherwise be carried on by the supported organizations? Explain why these activities would otherwise be carried on by the supported organizations.

9 Is the applicant organization controlled directly or indirectly by one or more "disqualified persons" (other than one who is a disqualified person solely because he or she is a manager) or by an organization that is not described in section 509(a)(1) or (2)? ☐ Yes ☐ No
If "Yes," explain.

Instructions

For an explanation of the types of organizations defined in section 509(a)(3) as being excluded from the definition of a private foundation, see Pub. 557, Chapter 3.

Line 1

List each organization that is supported by your organization and indicate in item **1b** if the supported organization has received a letter recognizing exempt status as a section 501(c)(3) public charity as defined in section 509(a)(1) or 509(a)(2). If you answer "No" in **1b** to any of the listed organizations, please explain in **1c.**

Line 3

Your organization's governing document may be articles of incorporation, articles of association, constitution, trust indenture, or trust agreement.

Line 9

For a definition of a "disqualified person," see **Specific Instructions,** Part II, Line 4d, on page 3 of the application's instructions.

Form 1023 (Rev. 9-98) Page **21**

Schedule E. Private Operating Foundations

	Income Test		Most recent tax year
1a	Adjusted net income, as defined in Regulations section 53.4942(a)-2(d)	1a	
b	Minimum investment return, as defined in Regulations section 53.4942(a)-2(c)	1b	
2	Qualifying distributions:		
a	Amounts (including administrative expenses) paid directly for the active conduct of the activities for which organized and operated under section 501(c)(3) (attach schedule)	2a	
b	Amounts paid to acquire assets to be used (or held for use) directly in carrying out purposes described in section 170(c)(1) or 170(c)(2)(B) (attach schedule)	2b	
c	Amounts set aside for specific projects that are for purposes described in section 170(c)(1) or 170(c)(2)(B) (attach schedule)	2c	
d	**Total** qualifying distributions (add lines 2a, b, and c)	2d	
3	Percentages:		
a	Percentage of qualifying distributions to adjusted net income (divide line 2d by line 1a)	3a	%
b	Percentage of qualifying distributions to minimum investment return (divide line 2d by line 1b). (Percentage must be at least 85% for 3a or 3b)	3b	%
	Assets Test		
4	Value of organization's assets used in activities that directly carry out the exempt purposes. Do not include assets held merely for investment or production of income (attach schedule)	4	
5	Value of any stock of a corporation that is controlled by applicant organization and carries out its exempt purposes (attach statement describing corporation)	5	
6	Value of all qualifying assets (add lines 4 and 5)	6	
7	Value of applicant organization's total assets	7	
8	Percentage of qualifying assets to total assets (divide line 6 by line 7—percentage must exceed 65%)	8	%
	Endowment Test		
9	Value of assets not used (or held for use) directly in carrying out exempt purposes:		
a	Monthly average of investment securities at fair market value	9a	
b	Monthly average of cash balances	9b	
c	Fair market value of all other investment property (attach schedule)	9c	
d	**Total** (add lines 9a, b, and c)	9d	
10	Acquisition indebtedness related to line 9 items (attach schedule)	10	
11	Balance (subtract line 10 from line 9d)	11	
12	Multiply line 11 by 3 1/3% (2/3 of the percentage for the minimum investment return computation under section 4942(e)). Line 2d above must equal or exceed the result of this computation	12	
	Support Test		
13	Applicant organization's support as defined in section 509(d)	13	
14	Gross investment income as defined in section 509(e)	14	
15	Support for purposes of section 4942(j)(3)(B)(iii) (subtract line 14 from line 13)	15	
16	Support received from the general public, five or more exempt organizations, or a combination of these sources (attach schedule)	16	
17	For persons (other than exempt organizations) contributing more than 1% of line 15, enter the total amounts that are more than 1% of line 15	17	
18	Subtract line 17 from line 16	18	
19	Percentage of total support (divide line 18 by line 15—must be at least 85%)	19	%
20	Does line 16 include support from an exempt organization that is more than 25% of the amount of line 15?	☐ Yes ☐ No	

21 Newly created organizations with less than 1 year's experience: Attach a statement explaining how the organization is planning to satisfy the requirements of section 4942(j)(3) for the income test and one of the supplemental tests during its first year's operation. Include a description of plans and arrangements, press clippings, public announcements, solicitations for funds, etc.

22 Does the amount entered on line 2a above include any grants that the applicant organization made? ☐ Yes ☐ No
If "Yes," attach a statement explaining how those grants satisfy the criteria for "significant involvement" grants described in section 53.4942(b)-1(b)(2) of the regulations.

For more information, see back of Schedule E.

Instructions

If the organization claims to be an operating foundation described in section 4942(j)(3) and—

a. Bases its claim to private operating foundation status on normal and regular operations over a period of years; or

b. Is newly created, set up as a private operating foundation, and has at least 1 year's experience;

provide the information under the **income test and under one of the three supplemental tests** (assets, endowment, or support). If the organization does not have at least 1 year's experience, provide the information called for on line 21. If the organization's private operating foundation status depends on its normal and regular operations as described in **a** above, attach a schedule similar to Schedule E showing the data in tabular form for the 3 years preceding the most recent tax year. (See Regulations section 53.4942(b)-1 for additional information before completing the "Income Test" section of this schedule.) Organizations claiming section 4942(j)(5) status must satisfy the income test and the endowment test.

A "private operating foundation" described in section 4942(j)(3) is a private foundation that spends substantially all of the smaller of its adjusted net income (as defined below) or its minimum investment return directly for the active conduct of the activities constituting the purpose or function for which it is organized and operated. The foundation must satisfy the income test under section 4942(j)(3)(A), as modified by Regulations section 53.4942(b)-1, and one of the following three supplemental tests: **(1)** the assets test under section 4942(j)(3)(B)(i); **(2)** the endowment test under section 4942(j)(3)(B)(ii); or **(3)** the support test under section 4942(j)(3)(B)(iii).

Certain long-term care facilities described in section 4942(j)(5) are treated as private operating foundations for purposes of section 4942 only.

"Adjusted net income" is the excess of gross income determined with the income modifications described below for the tax year over the sum of deductions determined with the deduction modifications described below. Items of gross income from any unrelated trade or business and the deductions directly connected with the unrelated trade or business are taken into account in computing the organization's adjusted net income.

Income Modifications

The following are income modifications (adjustments to gross income):

1. Section 103 (relating to interest on certain governmental obligations) does not apply. Thus, interest that otherwise would have been excluded should be included in gross income.

2. Except as provided in **3** below, capital gains and losses are taken into account only to the extent of the net short-term gain. Long-term gains and losses are disregarded.

3. The gross amount received from the sale or disposition of certain property should be included in gross income to the extent that the acquisition of the property constituted a qualifying distribution under section 4942(g)(1)(B).

4. Repayments of prior qualifying distributions (as defined in section 4942(g)(1)(A)) constitute items of gross income.

5. Any amount set aside under section 4942(g)(2) that is "not necessary for the purposes for which it was set aside" constitutes an item of gross income.

Deduction Modifications

The following are deduction modifications (adjustments to deductions):

1. Expenses for the general operation of the organization according to its charitable purposes (as contrasted with expenses for the production or collection of income and management, conservation, or maintenance of income-producing property) should not be taken as deductions. If only a portion of the property is used for production of income subject to section 4942 and the remainder is used for general charitable purposes, the expenses connected with that property should be divided according to those purposes. Only expenses related to the income-producing portion should be taken as deductions.

2. Charitable contributions, deductible under section 170 or 642(c), should not be taken into account as deductions for adjusted net income.

3. The net operating loss deduction prescribed under section 172 should not be taken into account as a deduction for adjusted net income.

4. The special deductions for corporations (such as the dividends-received deduction) allowed under sections 241 through 249 should not be taken into account as deductions for adjusted net income.

5. Depreciation and depletion should be determined in the same manner as under section 4940(c)(3)(B).

Section 265 (relating to the expenses and interest connected with tax-exempt income) should not be taken into account.

You may find it easier to figure adjusted net income by completing column (c), Part 1, Form 990-PF, according to the instructions for that form.

An organization that has been held to be a private operating foundation will continue to be such an organization only if it meets the income test and either the assets, endowment, or support test in later years. See Regulations section 53.4942(b) for additional information. No additional request for ruling will be necessary or appropriate for an organization to maintain its status as a private operating foundation. However, data related to the above tests must be submitted with the organization's annual information return, Form 990-PF.

Form 1023 (Rev. 9-98) Page 23

Schedule F. Homes for the Aged or Handicapped

1 What are the requirements for admission to residency? Explain fully and attach promotional literature and application forms.

2 Does or will the home charge an entrance or founder's fee? . . . . ☐ Yes ☐ No
If "Yes," explain and specify the amount charged.

3 What periodic fees or maintenance charges are or will be required of its residents?

4a What established policy does the home have concerning residents who become unable to pay their regular charges?

b What arrangements does the home have or will it make with local and Federal welfare units, sponsoring organizations, or others to absorb all or part of the cost of maintaining those residents?

5 What arrangements does or will the home have to provide for the health needs of its residents?

6 In what way are the home's residential facilities designed to meet some combination of the physical, emotional, recreational, social, religious, and similar needs of the aged or handicapped?

7 Provide a description of the home's facilities and specify both the residential capacity of the home and the current number of residents.

8 Attach a sample copy of the contract or agreement the organization makes with or requires of its residents.

For more information, see back of Schedule F.

Instructions

Line 1
Provide the criteria for admission to the home and submit brochures, pamphlets, or other printed material used to inform the public about the home's admissions policy.

Line 2
Indicate whether the fee charged is an entrance fee or a monthly charge, etc. Also, if the fee is an entrance fee, is it payable in a lump sum or on an installment basis?

Line 4
Indicate the organization's policy regarding residents who are unable to pay. Also, indicate whether the organization is subsidized for all or part of the cost of maintaining those residents who are unable to pay.

Line 5
Indicate whether the organization provides health care to the residents, either directly or indirectly, through some continuing arrangement with other organizations, facilities, or health personnel. If no health care is provided, indicate "N/A."

Schedule G. Child Care Organizations

1 Is the organization's primary activity the providing of care for children away from their homes?. . . . . ☐ **Yes** ☐ **No**

2 How many children is the organization authorized to care for by the state (or local governmental unit), and what was the average attendance during the past 6 months, or the number of months the organization has been in existence if less than 6 months?

3 How many children are currently cared for by the organization?

4 Is substantially all (at least 85%) of the care provided for the purpose of enabling parents to be gainfully employed or to seek employment? . . . ☐ **Yes** ☐ **No**

5 Are the services provided available to the general public?. . . . . ☐ **Yes** ☐ **No**
If "No," explain.

6 Indicate the category, or categories, of parents whose children are eligible for the child care services (check as many as apply):

☐ low-income parents

☐ any working parents (or parents looking for work)

☐ anyone with the ability to pay

☐ other (explain)

Instructions

Line 5
If your organization's services are not available to the general public, indicate the particular group or groups that may utilize the services.

REMINDER—If this organization claims to operate a school, then it must also fill out Schedule B.

Form 1023 (Rev. 9-98) Page **27**

Schedule H. Organizations Providing Scholarship Benefits, Student Aid, etc., to Individuals

1a Describe the nature and the amount of the scholarship benefit, student aid, etc., including the terms and conditions governing its use, whether a gift or a loan, and how the availability of the scholarship is publicized. If the organization has established or will establish several categories of scholarship benefits, identify each kind of benefit and explain how the organization determines the recipients for each category. Attach a sample copy of any application the organization requires individuals to complete to be considered for scholarship grants, loans, or similar benefits. (Private foundations that make grants for travel, study, or other similar purposes are required to obtain advance approval of scholarship procedures. See Regulations sections 53.4945-4(c) and (d).)

b If you want this application considered as a request for approval of grant procedures in the event we determine that the organization is a private foundation, check here . . . . ▶ ☐

c If you checked the box in **1b** above, check the box(es) for which you wish the organization to be considered.

☐ 4945(g)(1)   ☐ 4945(g)(2)   ☐ 4945(g)(3)

2 What limitations or restrictions are there on the class of individuals who are eligible recipients? Specifically explain whether there are, or will be, any restrictions or limitations in the selection procedures based upon race or the employment status of the prospective recipient or any relative of the prospective recipient. Also indicate the approximate number of eligible individuals.

3 Indicate the number of grants the organization anticipates making annually . . . . ▶

4 If the organization bases its selections in any way on the employment status of the applicant or any relative of the applicant, indicate whether there is or has been any direct or indirect relationship between the members of the selection committee and the employer. Also indicate whether relatives of the members of the selection committee are possible recipients or have been recipients.

5 Describe any procedures the organization has for supervising grants (such as obtaining reports or transcripts) that it awards and any procedures it has for taking action if the terms of the grant are violated.

For more information, see back of Schedule H.

Additional Information

Private foundations that make grants to individuals for travel, study, or other similar purposes are required to obtain advance approval of their grant procedures from the IRS. Such grants that are awarded under selection procedures that have not been approved by the IRS are subject to a 10% excise tax under section 4945. (See Regulations sections 53.4945-4(c) and (d).)

If you are requesting advance approval of the organization's grant procedures, the following sections apply to line **1c:**

4945(g)(1)— The grant constitutes a scholarship or fellowship grant that meets the provisions of section 117(a) prior to its amendment by the Tax Reform Act of 1986 and is to be used for study at an educational organization (school) described in section 170(b)(1)(A)(ii).

4945(g)(2)— The grant constitutes a prize or award that is subject to the provisions of section 74(b), if the recipient of such a prize or award is selected from the general public.

4945(g)(3)— The purpose of the grant is to achieve a specific objective, produce a report or other similar product, or improve or enhance a literary, artistic, musical, scientific, teaching, or other similar capacity, skill, or talent of the grantee.

Form 1023 (Rev. 9-98) Page **29**

Schedule I. Successors to "For Profit" Institutions

1 What was the name of the predecessor organization and the nature of its activities?

2 Who were the owners or principal stockholders of the predecessor organization? (If more space is needed, attach schedule.)

Name and address	Share or interest

3 Describe the business or family relationship between the owners or principal stockholders and principal employees of the predecessor organization and the officers, directors, and principal employees of the applicant organization.

4a Attach a copy of the agreement of sale or other contract that sets forth the terms and conditions of sale of the predecessor organization or of its assets to the applicant organization.

b Attach an appraisal by an independent qualified expert showing the fair market value at the time of sale of the facilities or property interest sold.

5 Has any property or equipment formerly used by the predecessor organization been rented to the applicant organization or will any such property be rented? ☐ Yes ☐ No
If "Yes," explain and attach copies of all leases and contracts.

6 Is the organization leasing or will it lease or otherwise make available any space or equipment to the owners, principal stockholders, or principal employees of the predecessor organization? ☐ Yes ☐ No
If "Yes," explain and attach a list of these tenants and a copy of the lease for each such tenant.

7 Were any new operating policies initiated as a result of the transfer of assets from a profit-making organization to a nonprofit organization? ☐ Yes ☐ No
If "Yes," explain.

Additional Information

A "for profit" institution for purposes of Schedule I includes any organization in which a person may have a proprietary or partnership interest, hold corporate stock, or otherwise exercise an ownership interest. The institution need not have operated for the purpose of making a profit.

Form **8718**
(Rev. November 2003)
Department of the Treasury
Internal Revenue Service

User Fee for Exempt Organization Determination Letter Request

▶ Attach this form to determination letter application.
(Form 8718 is NOT a determination letter application.)

For IRS Use Only

OMB No. 1545-1798
Control number _____
Amount paid _____
User fee screener

1 Name of organization	2 Employer Identification Number

Caution: *Do not attach Form 8718 to an application for a pension plan determination letter. Use Form 8717 instead.*

3 Type of request — Fee

a ☐ Initial request for a determination letter for:
- An exempt organization that has had annual gross receipts averaging not more than $10,000 during the preceding 4 years, or
- A new organization that anticipates gross receipts averaging not more than $10,000 during its first 4 years ▶ **$150**

Note: *If you checked box 3a, you must complete the Certification below.*

Certification

I certify that the annual gross receipts of ....
                                                                              name of organization
have averaged (or are expected to average) not more than $10,000 during the preceding 4 (or the first 4) years of operation.

Signature ▶   Title ▶

b ☐ Initial request for a determination letter for:
- An exempt organization that has had annual gross receipts averaging more than $10,000 during the preceding 4 years or
- A new organization that anticipates gross receipts averaging more than $10,000 during its first 4 years ▶ **$500**

c ☐ Group exemption letters . . . . ▶ **$500**

Instructions

The law requires payment of a user fee with each application for a determination letter. The user fees are listed on line 3 above. For more information, see Rev. Proc. 2003-8, 2003-1, I.R.B. 236, or latest annual update.

Check the box or boxes on line 3 for the type of application you are submitting. If you check box 3a, you must complete and sign the certification statement that appears under line 3a.

Attach to Form 8718 a check or money order payable to the "United States Treasury" for the full amount of the user fee. If you do not include the full amount, your application will be returned. Attach Form 8718 to your determination letter application.

Generally, the user fee will be refunded only if the Internal Revenue Service declines to issue a determination.

Where To File

Send the determination letter application and Form 8718 to:

Internal Revenue Service
P.O. Box 192
Covington, KY 41012-0192

If you are using express mail or a delivery service, send the application and Form 8718 to:

Internal Revenue Service
201 West Rivercenter Blvd.
Attn: Extracting Stop 312
Covington, KY 41011

Paperwork Reduction Act Notice. We ask for the information on this form to carry out the Internal Revenue laws of the United States. If you want your organization to be recognized as tax-exempt by the IRS, you are required to give us this information. We need it to determine whether the organization meets the legal requirements for tax-exempt status.

You are not required to provide the information requested on a form that is subject to the Paperwork Reduction Act unless the form displays a valid OMB control number. Books or records relating to a form or its instructions must be retained as long as their contents may become material in the administration of any Internal Revenue law. The rules governing the confidentiality of Form 8718 are covered in Code section 6104.

The time needed to complete and file this form will vary depending on individual circumstances. The estimated average time is 5 minutes. If you have comments concerning the accuracy of this time estimate or suggestions for making this form simpler, we would be happy to hear from you. You can write to the Tax Products Coordinating Committee, Western Area Distribution Center, Rancho Cordova, CA 95743-0001. **Do not** send this form to this address. Instead, see **Where To File** above.

Attach Check or Money Order Here

Cat. No. 64728Z

Form **2848**
(Rev. January 2002)
Department of the Treasury
Internal Revenue Service

Power of Attorney and Declaration of Representative

▶ See the separate instructions.

OMB No. 1545-0150

For IRS Use Only
Received by:
Name _____
Telephone _____
Function _____
Date __/__/__

Part I Power of Attorney (Type or print.)

1 Taxpayer information. Taxpayer(s) must sign and date this form on page 2, line 9.

Taxpayer name(s) and address	Social security number(s)	Employer identification number
	Daytime telephone number ( )	Plan number (if applicable)

hereby appoint(s) the following representative(s) as attorney(s)-in-fact:

2 Representative(s) must sign and date this form on page 2, Part II.

Name and address	CAF No. .... Telephone No. .... Fax No. .... Check if new: Address ☐ Telephone No. ☐
Name and address	CAF No. .... Telephone No. .... Fax No. .... Check if new: Address ☐ Telephone No. ☐
Name and address	CAF No. .... Telephone No. .... Fax No. .... Check if new: Address ☐ Telephone No. ☐

to represent the taxpayer(s) before the Internal Revenue Service for the following tax matters:

3 Tax matters

Type of Tax (Income, Employment, Excise, etc.) or Civil Penalty (See the instructions for line 3.)	Tax Form Number (1040, 941, 720, etc.)	Year(s) or Period(s)

4 Specific use not recorded on Centralized Authorization File (CAF). If the power of attorney is for a specific use not recorded on CAF, check this box. See the instructions for **Line 4. Specific uses not recorded on CAF.** . . . . ▶ ☐

5 Acts authorized. The representatives are authorized to receive and inspect confidential tax information and to perform any and all acts that I (we) can perform with respect to the tax matters described on line 3, for example, the authority to sign any agreements, consents, or other documents. The authority does not include the power to receive refund checks (see line 6 below), the power to substitute another representative, the authority to execute a request for a tax return, or a consent to disclose tax information unless specifically added below, or the power to sign certain returns. See the instructions for **Line 5. Acts authorized.**

List any specific additions or deletions to the acts otherwise authorized in this power of attorney: _____
_____
_____

Note: *In general, an unenrolled preparer of tax returns cannot sign any document for a taxpayer. See Revenue Procedure 81-38, printed as Pub. 470, for more information.*

Note: *The tax matters partner of a partnership is not permitted to authorize representatives to perform certain acts. See the separate instructions for more information.*

6 Receipt of refund checks. If you want to authorize a representative named on line 2 to receive, **BUT NOT TO ENDORSE OR CASH**, refund checks, initial here _____ and list the name of that representative below.

Name of representative to receive refund check(s) ▶

For Paperwork Reduction and Privacy Act Notice, see the separate instructions.   Cat. No. 11980J   Form **2848** (Rev. 1-2002)

Form 2848 (Rev. 1-2002) Page **2**

7 Notices and communications. Original notices and other written communications will be sent to you and a copy to the first representative listed on line 2 unless you check one or more of the boxes below.
  a If you want the first representative listed on line 2 to receive the original, and yourself a copy, of such notices or communications, check this box . . . . ▶ ☐
  b If you also want the second representative listed to receive a copy of such notices and communications, check this box. ▶ ☐
  c If you do not want any notices or communications sent to your representative(s), check this box . . . . ▶ ☐

8 Retention/revocation of prior power(s) of attorney. The filing of this power of attorney automatically revokes all earlier power(s) of attorney on file with the Internal Revenue Service for the same tax matters and years or periods covered by this document. If you **do not** want to revoke a prior power of attorney, check here. . . . . ▶ ☐
  YOU MUST ATTACH A COPY OF ANY POWER OF ATTORNEY YOU WANT TO REMAIN IN EFFECT.

9 Signature of taxpayer(s). If a tax matter concerns a joint return, **both** husband and wife must sign if joint representation is requested, otherwise, see the instructions. If signed by a corporate officer, partner, guardian, tax matters partner, executor, receiver, administrator, or trustee on behalf of the taxpayer, I certify that I have the authority to execute this form on behalf of the taxpayer.

  ▶ **IF NOT SIGNED AND DATED, THIS POWER OF ATTORNEY WILL BE RETURNED.**

Signature	Date	Title (if applicable)
Print Name		
Signature	Date	Title (if applicable)
Print Name		

Part II Declaration of Representative

Caution: *Students with a special order to represent taxpayers in Qualified Low Income Taxpayer Clinics or the Student Tax Clinic Program, see the separate instructions for Part II.*

Under penalties of perjury, I declare that:
- I am not currently under suspension or disbarment from practice before the Internal Revenue Service;
- I am aware of regulations contained in Treasury Department Circular No. 230 (31 CFR, Part 10), as amended, concerning the practice of attorneys, certified public accountants, enrolled agents, enrolled actuaries, and others;
- I am authorized to represent the taxpayer(s) identified in Part I for the tax matter(s) specified there; and
- I am one of the following:
  a Attorney- a member in good standing of the bar of the highest court of the jurisdiction shown below.
  b Certified Public Accountant- duly qualified to practice as a certified public accountant in the jurisdiction shown below.
  c Enrolled Agent- enrolled as an agent under the requirements of Treasury Department Circular No. 230.
  d Officer- a bona fide officer of the taxpayer's organization.
  e Full-Time Employee- a full-time employee of the taxpayer.
  f Family Member- a member of the taxpayer's immediate family (i.e., spouse, parent, child, brother, or sister).
  g Enrolled Actuary- enrolled as an actuary by the Joint Board for the Enrollment of Actuaries under 29 U.S.C. 1242 (the authority to practice before the Service is limited by section 10.3(d)(1) of Treasury Department Circular No. 230).
  h Unrolled Return Preparer- an unenrolled return preparer under section 10.7(c)(1)(viii) of Treasury Department Circular No. 230.

▶ **IF THIS DECLARATION OF REPRESENTATIVE IS NOT SIGNED AND DATED, THE POWER OF ATTORNEY WILL BE RETURNED.**

Designation- Insert above letter **(a- h)**	Jurisdiction (state) or Enrollment Card No.	Signature	Date

Form **2848** (Rev. 1-2002)

Checklist for Completing IRS Form 1023

Make sure to attach and send the following items along with your Form 1023:

Checklist (Do not send this to the IRS)

- ☐ Articles of Incorporation - Approved Copy from the state
- ☐ Articles of Amendment (if applicable) - Approved Copy
- ☐ Bylaws - Adopted & Signed
- ☐ Copy of your EIN application and approval from IRS
- ☐ List of any assets and their total value
- ☐ Programs brochure or flyer (if applicable)
- ☐ List of Directors or Officers w/names, addresses, salaries (if any)
- ☐ Property lease (if applicable)
- ☐ Copy of Order of Service (for churches)
- ☐ Form 8718
- ☐ Form 872-C (two copies)

Where to Send Your Application: Internal Revenue Service, P.O. Box 192, Covington, KY 41012-0192

Applications shipped by express mail or delivery service should be sent to : Internal Revenue Service, 201 W. Rivercenter Blvd., Attn: Extracting Stop 312, Covington, KY 41011

WHERE TO GET INFORMATION ON NONPROFIT CORPORATION LAWS AND FORMS IN EVERY STATE

Alabama
Secretary of State
Corporate Division

P.O. Box 5616
Montgomery, AL 36103-5616
www.sos.state.al.us/
334-242-5324

Alaska
Corporate Division
Department of Commerce & Economic Development
P.O. Box 110505
Juneau, AK 99811-0808
www.dced.state.ak.us/
907-465-2530

Arizona
Corporation Commission
1300 West Washington
Phoenix, AZ 85007-2996
www.az.gov/wepbapp/portal
602-542-3026

Arkansas
Aegon Building, Suite 310
501 Woodland
Little Rock, AR 72201-1010
www.state.ar.us
501-682-3409

California
Secretary of State
1500 11th Street
Sacramento, CA 95814
www.state.ca/us/state/portal/myca_homepage.jsp
916-657-5448

Colorado
Secretary of State
Commercial Recording Division
1560 Broadway, Suite 200
Denver, CO 80202
www.state.co.us/
303-894-2251

Connecticut
Secretary of State
30 Trinity St.
Hartford, CT 06106
www.ct.gov
860-509-6079

Delaware
Department of State
Divisions of Corporation
P.O. Box 898
Dover, DE 19903
www.state.de.us/
302-739-3073

District of Columbia
Division of Consumer &
Regulatory Affairs
Corporations Divisions
941 N. Capitol Street NE
Washington, DC 20002
www.dc.gov
202-442-4430

Georgia
Secretary of State
Corporations Division
315 West Tower
#2 Martin Luther King Jr. Drive
Atlanta, GA 30334
www.state.ga.us/
404-656-2817

Idaho
Secretary of State
700 West Jefferson
P.O. Box 83720
Boise, ID 83720-0080
www.state.id.us/
208-334-2301

Indiana
Secretary of State
Business Service Division
302 W. Washington Street
Room E018
Indianapolis, IN 46204
www.state.in.us/
317-232-6576

Florida
Secretary of State
Division of Corporations
P.O. Box 6327
Tallahassee, FL 32314
www.state.fl.us
850-422-9000

Hawaii
Division of Commerce & Consumer Affairs
Business Registration Division
305 Merchant Street, 2nd Floor
P.O. Box 40
Honolulu, HI 96810
www.state.hi.us
808-586-2727

Illinois
Secretary of State
Business Services Department
Corporation Division
Howlett Building, Third Floor
Springfield, IL 62756
www.state.il.us/
217-782-6961

Iowa
Secretary of State
Corporations Division
Lucas Building, 1st Floor
Des Moines, IA 50319
www.state.ia.us
515-281-5204

Kansas
Secretary of State
2nd Floor, State Capitol
300 S.W. 10th Ave.
Topeka, KS 6612-1594
www.accesskansas.org
785-296-4564

Kentucky
Office of the Secretary of State
Business Filings
State Capitol Building, Room 154
700 Capital Avenue
Frankfort, KY 40604
www.kydirect.net
502-564-3490

Louisiana
Secretary of State
Corporate Division
P.O. Box 94125
Baton, Rouge, LA 70804
www.state.la.us
225-925-4704

Maine
Secretary of State
Bureau of Corporations, Elections and Commissions
101 State House Section
Augusta, ME 04333-0101
www.state.me.us
207-624-7740

Maryland
State Department of Assessments and Taxation
Corporate Charter Divisions
301 West Preston Street
Baltimore, MD 21201
www.state.md.us/
410-767-1340

Massachusetts
Corporation Division
Secretary of the Commonwealth
One Ashburton Place, Room 1717
Boston, MA 02108
www.mass.gov/portal/index.jsp
617-727-9640

Michigan
Michigan Department of
Consumer & Industry Services
Corporation Division
P.O. Box 30054
Lansing, MI 48909-7554
www.michigan.gov
514-241-6400

Minnesota
Secretary of State
Business Services Division
180 State Office Blvd.
100 Constitution Avenue
Saint Paul, MN 55146
www.state.mn.us/
651-296-2803

Mississippi
Office of the Mississippi
Secretary of State
P.O. Box 136
Jackson, MS 39205-1633
www.msn.gov
601-359-1633
1-800-256-3494

Montana
Secretary of State
Business Service Bureau
P.O. Box 202801
Helena, MT 59620-2801
www.mt.us/css/default.asp
406-444-3665

Nevada
Customer Service Division
Capitol Complex
101 N. Carson St., Suite 3
Carson City, NV 89701-4786
http://silver.state.nv.us/
775-684-5708

New Jersey
New Jersey Division of Revenue
Corporate Filing Unit
225 W. State Street
P.O. Box 308
Trenton, NJ 08625-0308
www.state.nj.us/
609-292-9292

Missouri
Secretary of State
Corporation Division
P.O. Box 778
Jefferson City, MO 65102
www.state.mo.us/
573-751-4153

Nebraska
Secretary of State
Corporations Division
Suite 1305
P.O. Box 94608
Lincoln, NE 68509-4608
www.state.ne.us/
402-471-4079

New Hampshire
Secretary of State
Corporation Divisions
State House
107 N. Main Street
Concord, NH 03301-4989
www.state.nh.us/
603-271-3244

New Mexico
State Corporation Commission
Corporation Department
P.O. Box 1296
Sante Fe, NM 87504-1269
www.state.nm.us/
505-827-4511

New York
Department of State
Division of Corporation
41 State Street
Albany, NY 12231-0001
www.state.ny.us/
518-473-2492

North Dakota
Secretary of State
Business Division Department 108
600 East Boulevard Avenue
Bismarck, ND 58505-0500
www.discovernd.com
701-328-4284

Oklahoma
Secretary of State
101 State Capitol
2300 North Lincoln Blvd.
Oklahoma City, OK 73118
www.state.ok.us/
405-521-3911 (forms)
405-522-4560 (info)

Pennsylvania
Department of State
Corporations Bureau
308 North Office Building
Harrisburg, PA 17120-0029
www.state.pa.us/papower
717-787-1057

South Carolina
Secretary of State
P.O. Box 11350
Columbia, SC 29211
www.myscgov.com
803-734-2158

North Carolina
Corporations Division
Department of Secretary of State
P.O. Box 29622
Raleigh, NC 27626-0622
www.ncgov.com
919-807-2225

Ohio
Secretary of State
Business Services
30 East Broad Street, 14th Floor
Columbus, OH 43266
www.state.oh.us/
614–466-2623

Oregon
Secretary of State
Corporations Division
255 Capitol Street, NE Suite 151
Salem, OR 97310-1327
www.oregon.gov
503-986-2200

Rhode Island
Secretary of State
Corporation of State
100 N. Main Street
Providence, RI 02903
www.state.ri.us/
401-222-3040

South Dakota
Secretary of State
State Capitol
500 E. Capitol
Pierre, SD 57501-5077
www.state.sd.us/
605-773-4550

Tennessee
Department of State
Division of Business Services
312 Eighth Avenue North
6th Floor William R. Snodgrass Tower
Nashville, TN 37243
www.state.tn.us/
615-741-2286

Utah
Department of Commerce &
Commercial Code
Heber M. Wells Building
160 East 300 South
P.O. Box 45802
Salt Lake City, UT 84145-0802
www.utah.gov
801-530-4849

Virginia
Clerk's Information Office
State Corporations Commission
Tyler Building
1300 East Main Street
P.O. Box 1197
Richmond, VA 23218-1197
www.state.va.us/
804-371-9676

West Virginia
Secretary of State
Corporations Division
State Capitol, W-139
1900 Kanawha Blvd. East
Charleston, WV 25305-0770
www.state.wv.us/
304-558-8000

Texas
Secretary of State
Business & Public Filing Division
Corporation Section
P.O. Box 13697
Austin, TX 78711-3697
www.state.tx.us/
512-463-5555

Vermont
Secretary of State
Division of Corporations
81 River Street, Drawer 09
Heritage Building
Montpelier, VT 05609-1104
www.state.vt.us/
802-828-2386

Washington
Office of the Secretary of State
Corporations Divisions
P.O. Box 40234
Olympia, WA 98504-0234
http://access.wa.gov
360-753-7115

Wisconsin
Department of Financial Institutions
Division of Corporate & Consumer Services
P.O. Box 7846
Madison, WI 53707-7846
www.wisconsin.gov
608-261-7577

Wyoming
Secretary of State
Corporations Division
State Capitol
Cheyenne, WY 82002-0020
www.state.wy.us/
307-777-7311/7312

THE BEST GUIDE FOR NONPROFIT CORPORATIONS

State Nonprofit Corporation Fees

Each state requires application. Below is a list of basic fees. Additional fees may be asked for certified copies of your documents. If you make changes to your initial documents, you will be required to pay a fee to amend your articles.

State	Fee	State	Fee
Alabama	$100	Missouri	$ 35
Alaska	50	Montana	40
Arizona	75	Nebraska	20
Arkansas	50	Nevada	25
California	30	New Hampshire	55
Colorado	30	New Jersey	110
Connecticut	65	New Mexico	25
Delaware	74	New York	130
District of Columbia	80	North Carolina	60
Florida	70	North Dakota	30
Georgia	100	Ohio	125
Hawaii	50	Oklahoma	25
Idaho	50	Oregon	20
Illinois	57	Pennsylvania	100
Indiana	30	Rhode Island	35
Iowa	20	South Carolina	25
Kansas	40	South Dakota	25
Kentucky	8	Tennessee	100
Louisiana	100	Texas	50
Maine	5	Utah	20
Maryland	40	Vermont	75
Massachusetts	35	Virginia	80
Michigan	20	Washington	70
Minnesota	90	West Virginia	25
Mississippi	50	Wisconsin	60
		Wyoming	25

THE BEST GUIDE FOR NONPROFIT CORPORATIONS

Tax Guide for Churches and Religious Organizations

This section of the book came directly from the IRS. I felt that it was important to include this guide, because it contains valuable information that many religious organizations are not aware of, such as how they could jeopardize their tax-exempt status, unrelated business income tax or parsonage or housing allowances. There are many other items discussed in this chapter. Once your organization has this knowledge, it will operate more proficiently.

THE BEST GUIDE FOR NONPROFIT CORPORATIONS

IRS TAX GUIDE

for

CHURCHES

and

RELIGIOUS ORGANIZATIONS

Publication 1828 (Rev. 7-2002)

Catalog No. 21096G

Congress has enacted special tax laws applicable to churches, religious organizations, and ministers in recognition of their unique status in American society and of their rights guaranteed by the First Amendment of the Constitution of the United States. Churches and religious organizations are generally exempt from income tax and receive other favorable treatment under the tax law; however, certain income of a church or religious organization may be subject to tax, such as income from an unrelated business. It is also important for a church or religious organization to understand the tax law to avoid losing its tax-exempt status by engaging in activity that violates the Internal Revenue Code.

The Internal Revenue Service offers this quick reference guide for federal tax law and procedures for churches and religious organizations to help them voluntarily comply with tax rules. The contents of this publication reflect the IRS' interpretation of tax laws enacted by Congress, Treasury regulations, and court decisions. The information given is not comprehensive, however, and does not cover every situation. Thus, it is not intended to replace the law or be the sole source of information. The resolution of any particular issue may depend on the specific facts and circumstances of a given taxpayer. In addition, this publication covers subjects on which a court may have made a decision more favorable to taxpayers than the interpretation by the IRS. Until these differing interpretations are resolved by higher court decisions, or in some other way, this publication will present the interpretation of the IRS.

For more detailed tax information, the IRS has assistance programs and tax information products for churches and religious organization, as noted in the back of this publication.

Most IRS publications and forms can be downloaded from the IRS Web site at www.irs.gov, or ordered by calling toll-free (800) 820-3767. Specialized information can be accessed through the Exempt Organizations Web site under the IRS Tax Exempt and Government Entities division via www.irs.gov/eo or by calling toll-free (877) 829-5500.

The IRS considers this publication a living document, one that will be revised to take into account future developments and feedback. Comments on the publication may be submitted to the IRS at the following address:Internal Revenue Service, 1111 Constitution Avenue NW, Washington, DC 20224, attn: T:EO:CE&O

CONTENTS

Tax-Exempt Status... 139

Recognition of Tax-Exempt Status

Applying for Tax-Exempt Status

Public Listing of Tax-Exempt Organizations

Jeopardizing Tax-Exempt Status 142

Inurement and Private Benefit

Substantial Lobbying Activity

Political Campaign Activity

Unrelated Business Income Tax (UBIT) 153

Net Income Subject to the UBIT

Examples of Unrelated Trade or Business Activities

Tax on Income-Producing Activities

Employment Tax 156

Social Security and Medicare Taxes

Federal Insurance Contributions Act (FICA)

Federal Unemployment Tax Act (FUTA)

Special Rules for Compensation of Ministers **158**

Withholding Income Tax for Ministers

Parsonage or Housing Allowances

Social Security and Medicare Taxes

Federal Insurance Contributions Act (FICA) vs. SECA
(Self-Employment Contributions Act) Tax

Payment of Employee, Business Expenses **160**

Accountable Reimbursement Plan On-accountable Reimbursement Plan

Record Keeping Requirements **162**

Books of Accounting and Other Types of Records

Length of Time to Retain Records

Filing Requirements **163**

Information and Tax Returns

Forms to File and Due Dates

Charitable Contributions—Substantiation and Disclosure Rules **167**

Substantiation Rules

Disclosure Rules That Apply to *Quid Pro Quo* Contributions

Exceptions to Disclosure Statement

Special Rules Limiting IRS Authority to Audit a Church **168**

Tax Inquiries and Examinations of Churches

Audit Process

Glossary 171

Help from the IRS 173

IRS Tax Publications to Order

This publication explains the benefits and the responsibilities under the federal tax system for churches and religious organizations. The term *church* is found, but not specifically defined, in the Internal Revenue Code. The term is not used by all faiths; however, in an attempt to make this publication easy to read, we use it in its generic sense as a place of worship including, for example, mosques and synagogues. With the exception of the special rules for church audits, the use of the term *church* throughout this publication also includes conventions and associations of churches, as well as integrated auxiliaries of a church.

Because special tax rules apply to churches, it is important to distinguish churches from other religious organizations. Therefore, when this publication uses the term *religious organizations*, it is not referring to churches or integrated auxiliaries. Religious organizations that are not churches typically include nondenominational ministries, interdenominational and ecumenical organizations, and other entities whose principal purpose is the study or advancement of religion.

Churches and religious organizations may be legally organized in a variety of ways under state law, such as unincorporated associations, nonprofit corporations, corporations sole, and charitable trusts.

Certain terms used throughout this publication – *church, integrated auxiliary of a church, minister,* and IRC Section 501(C)(3)— are defined in the Glossary on page 221.

TAX-EXEMPT STATUS

Churches and religious organizations, like many other charitable organizations, qualify for exemption from federal income tax under IRC Section 501(C)(3) and are generally eligible to receive tax-deductible contributions. To qualify for tax-exempt status, such an organization must meet the following requirements (covered in greater detail throughout this publication):

- the organization must be organized and operated exclusively for religious, educational, scientific, or other charitable purposes,

- net earnings may not inure to the benefit of any private individual or shareholder,

- no substantial part of its activity may be attempting to influence legislation,

- the organization may not intervene in political campaigns, and

- the organization's purposes and activities may not be illegal or violate fundamental public policy.

Recognition of Tax-Exempt Status

Automatic Exemption for Churches

Churches that meet the requirements of IRC Section 501(C)(3) are automatically considered tax exempt and are not required to apply for and obtain recognition of tax-exempt status from the IRS.

Although there is no requirement to do so, many churches seek recognition of tax-exempt status from the IRS because such recognition assures church leaders, members, and contributors that the church is recognized as exempt and qualifies for related tax benefits. For example, contributors to a church that has been recognized as tax exempt would know that their contributions generally are tax deductible.

Church Exemption through a Central/Parent Organization

A church with a parent organization may wish to contact the parent to see if it has a group ruling. If the parent holds a group ruling, then the IRS may already recognize the church as tax exempt. Under the group exemption process, the parent organization becomes the holder of a group ruling that identifies other affiliated churches or other affiliated organizations. A church is recognized as tax exempt if it is included in a list provided by the parent organization. The parent is then required to submit an annual group-exemption update to the IRS in which it provides additions, deletions, and changes within the group. If the church or other affiliated organization is included on such a list, it does not need to take further action to obtain recognition of tax-exempt status. An organization that is not covered under a group ruling should contact its parent organization to see if it is eligible to be included in the parent's application for the group ruling. For general information on the group-exemption process, see Revenue Procedure 80-27, 1980-1 C.B. 677.

Religious Organizations

Unlike churches, religious organizations that wish to be tax exempt generally must apply to the IRS for tax-exempt status unless their gross receipts do not normally exceed $5,000 annually.

Applying for Tax-Exempt Status

Employer Identification Number (EIN)

Every tax-exempt organization, including a church, should have an employer identification number (EIN), whether or not the organization has any employees. There are many instances in which an EIN is necessary. For example, a church needs an EIN when it opens a bank account, in order to be listed as a subordinate in a group ruling, or if it files returns with the IRS (e.g., Forms W-2, 1099, 990-T.)

An organization that does not have an EIN should file Form SS-4, *Application for Employer Identification Number*, in accordance with the instructions. If the organization is submitting IRS Form 1023, *Application for Recognition of Exemption Under Section 501(C)(3) of the Internal Revenue Code* (see below), Form SS-4 should be included with the application.

Application Form

Organizations, including churches and religious organizations, that wish to be recognized as tax exempt under IRC Section 501(C)(3) must use Form 1023.

A religious organization must submit its application within 27 months from the end of the month in which the organization is formed in order to be considered tax exempt and qualified to receive deductible contributions as of the date the organization was formed. On the other hand, a church may obtain recognition of exemption for time periods prior to the date of its request for tax-exempt status, even if it does not submit its application within 27 months of formation.

Cost for applying for exemption. The IRS is required to collect a non-refundable fee from any organization seeking a determination of tax-exempt status under IRC Section 501(C)(3.) Although churches are not required by law to file an application for exemption, if they choose to do so voluntarily, they are required to pay the fee for determination.

The fee must be submitted with Form 1023; otherwise, the application will be returned to the sumiter. Fees change periodically and are listed on IRS Form 8718, *User Fee for Exempt Organization Determination Letter Request*, which is used to transmit both the appropriate fee and the application for exemption. The most recent user fee can be found at the Exempt Organizations (EO) Web site under the IRS Tax Exempt and Government Entities division via www.irs.gov/eo or by calling EO Customer Account Services toll-free at (877)829-5500.

IRS Approval of Exemption Application

If the application for tax-exempt status is approved, the IRS will notify the organization of its status, any requirement to file an annual information return, and its eligibility to receive deductible contributions. The IRS does not assign a special number or other identification as evidence of an organization's tax-exempt status.

Public Listing of Tax-Exempt Organizations

The IRS lists organizations that are qualified to receive tax-deductible contributions in IRS Publication 78, *Cumulative List of Organizations Described in Section 170(c) of the Internal Revenue Code of 1986*. This publication is sold to the public through the Superintendent of Documents, U.S. Government Printing Office, Washington, DC. Publication 78 can also be downloaded from the IRS Web site at www.irs.gov. Note that not every organization that is eligible to receive tax-deductible contributions is listed in Publication 78. For example, churches that have not applied for recognition of tax-exempt status are not included in the publication. Only the parent organization in a group ruling is included by name in Publication 78. If you have questions about listing an organization, correcting an erroneous entry, or deleting a listing in Publication 78, contact EO Customer Account Services toll-free at (877) 829-5500.

JEOPARDIZING TAX-EXEMPT STATUS

All IRC Section 501(C)(3) organizations, including churches and religious organizations, must abide by certain rules:

- Their net earnings may not inure to any private shareholder or individual,

- They must not provide a substantial benefit to private interests,

- They must not devote a substantial part of their activities to attempting to influence legislation,

- They must not participate in, or intervene in, any political campaign on behalf of (or in opposition to) any candidate for public office, and

- The organization's purposes and activities may not be illegal or violate fundamental public policy.

Inurement and Private Benefit

Inurement to Insiders

Churches and religious organizations, like all exempt organizations under IRC Section 501(C)(3), are prohibited from engaging in activities that result in inurement of the church's or organization's income or assets to insiders (i.e., persons having a personal and private interest in the activities of the organization.) *Insiders* could include the minister, church board members, officers, and, in certain circumstances, employees. Examples of prohibited inurement include the payment of dividends, the payment of unreasonable compensation to insiders, and transferring property to insiders for less than fair market value. The prohibition against inurement to insiders is absolute; therefore, any amount of inurement is, potentially, grounds for loss of tax-exempt status. In addition, the insider involved may be subject to excise tax. See the following section on *excess benefit transactions*. Note that prohibited inurement does not include reasonable payments for services rendered, payments that further tax-exempt purposes, or payments made for the fair market value of real or personal property.

Excess benefit transactions. In cases where an IRC Section 501(C)(3) organization provides an excess economic benefit to an insider, both the organization and the insider have engaged in an *excess benefit transaction*. The IRS may impose an excise tax on any insider who improperly benefits from an excess benefit transaction, as well as on organization managers who participate in such a transaction knowing that it is improper. An insider who benefits from an excess benefit transaction is also required to return the excess benefits to the organization. Detailed rules on excess benefit transactions are contained in the Code of Federal Regulations,

Title 26, sections 53.4958-0 through 53.4958-8.

Private Benefit

An IRC Section 501(C)(3) organization's activities must be directed exclusively toward charitable, educational, religious, or other exempt purposes. Such an organization's activities may not serve the private interests of any individual or organization. Rather, beneficiaries of an organization's activities must be recognized objects of charity (such as the poor or the distressed) or the community at large (for example, through the conduct of religious services or the promotion of religion.) Private benefit is different from inurement to insiders. Private benefit may occur even if the persons benefitted are not insiders. Also, private benefit must be substantial in order to jeopardize tax-exempt status.

Substantial Lobbying Activity

In general, no organization, including a church, may qualify for IRC Section 501(C)(3) status if a substantial part of its activities is attempting to influence legislation (commonly known as lobbying.) An IRC Section 501(C)(3) organization may engage in some lobbying, but too much lobbying activity risks loss of tax-exempt status.

Legislation includes action by Congress, any state legislature, any local council, or similar governing body, with respect to acts, bills, resolutions, or similar items (such as legislative confirmation of appointive offices), or by the public in a referendum, ballot initiative, constitutional amendment, or similar procedure. It does not include actions by executive, judicial, or administrative bodies.

A church or religious organization will be regarded as *attempting to influence legislation* if it contacts, or urges the public to contact, members or employees of a legislative body for the purpose of proposing, supporting, or opposing legislation, or if the organization advocates the adoption or rejection of legislation.

Churches and religious organizations may, however, involve themselves in issues of public policy without the activity being considered as lobbying. For example, churches may conduct educational meetings, prepare and distribute educational materials, or otherwise consider public policy issues in an educational manner without jeopardizing their tax-exempt status.

Measuring Lobbying Activity

Substantial part test. Whether a church's or religious organization's attempts to influence legislation constitute a substantial part of its overall activities is determined on the basis of all the pertinent facts and circumstances in each case. The IRS considers a variety of factors, including the time devoted (by both compensated and volunteer workers) and the expenditures devoted by the organization to the activity, when determining whether the lobbying activity is substantial. Churches must use the substantial part test since they are not eligible to use the expenditure test described in the next section.

Consequences of excessive lobbying activity. Under the *substantial part test*, a church or religious organization that conducts excessive lobbying activity in any taxable year may lose its tax-exempt status, resulting in all of its income being subject to tax. In addition, a religious organization is subject to an excise tax equal to 5% of its lobbying expenditures for the year in which it ceases to qualify for exemption. Further, a tax equal to 5% of the lobbying expenditures for the year may be imposed against organization managers, jointly and severally, who agree to the making of such expenditures knowing that the expenditures would likely result in loss of tax-exempt status.

Expenditure test. Although churches are not eligible, religious organizations may elect the expenditure test under IRC Section 501(h) as an alternative method for measuring lobbying activity. Under the expenditure test, the extent of an organization's lobbying activity will not jeopardize its tax-exempt status, provided its expenditures, related to such activity, do not normally exceed an amount specified in IRC Section 4911. This limit is generally based upon the size of the organization and may not exceed $1,000,000.

Religious organizations electing to use the expenditure test must file IRS Form 5768, *Election/Revocation of Election by an Eligible IRC Section 501(C)(3) Organization To Make Expenditures To Influence Legislation*, at any time during the tax year for which it is to be effective. The election remains in effect for succeeding years unless it is revoked by the organization. Revocation of the election is effective beginning with the year following the year in which the revocation is filed. Religious organizations may wish to consult their tax advisors to determine their eligibility for, and the advisability of, electing the expenditure test.

Consequences of excessive lobbying activity. Under the *expenditure test*, a religious organization that engages in excessive lobbying activity over a four-year period may lose its tax-exempt status, making all of its income for that period subject to tax. Should the organization exceed its lobbying expenditure dollar limit in a particular year, it must pay an excise tax equal to 25% of the excess.

Political Campaign Activity

Under the Internal Revenue Code, all IRC Section 501(C)(3) organizations, including churches and religious organizations, are absolutely prohibited from directly or indirectly participating in, or intervening in, any political campaign on behalf of (or in opposition to) any candidate for elective public office. Contributions to political campaign funds or public statements of position (verbal or written) made by or on behalf of the organization in favor of or in opposition to any candidate for public office clearly violate the prohibition against political campaign activity. Violation of this prohibition may result in denial or revocation of tax-exempt status and the imposition of certain excise tax.

Certain activities or expenditures may not be prohibited depending on the facts and circumstances. For example, certain voter education activities (including the presentation of public forums and the publication of voter education guides) conducted in a non-partisan manner do not constitute prohibited political campaign activity. In addition, other activities intended to encourage people to participate in the electoral process, such as voter registration and get-out-the-vote drives, would not constitute prohibited political campaign activity if conducted in a non-partisan manner. On the other hand, voter education or registration activities with evidence of bias that (a) would favor one candidate over another; (b) oppose a candidate in some manner; or (c) have the effect of favoring a candidate or group of candidates, will constitute prohibited participation or intervention.

Individual Activity by Religious Leaders

The political campaign activity prohibition is not intended to restrict free expression on political matters by leaders of churches or religious organizations speaking for themselves, as *individuals*. Nor are leaders prohibited from speaking about important issues of public policy. However, for their organizations to remain tax exempt under IRC Section 501(C)(3), religious leaders cannot make partisan comments in official organization publications or at official church functions. To avoid potential attribution of their comments outside of church functions and publications, religious leaders who speak or write in their individual capacity are encouraged to clearly indicate that their comments are personal and not intended to represent the views of the organization. The following are examples of situations involving endorsements by religious leaders.

> *Example 1:* Minister A is the minister of Church J and is well known in the community. With their permission, Candidate T publishes a full-page ad in the local newspaper listing five prominent ministers who have personally endorsed Candidate T, including Minister A. Minister A is identified in the ad as the minister of Church J. The ad states, "Titles and affiliations of each individual are provided for identification purposes only." The ad is paid for by Candidate T's campaign committee. Since the ad was not paid for by Church J, the ad is not otherwise in an official publication of Church J, and since the endorsement is made by Minister A in a personal capacity, the ad does not constitute campaign intervention by Church J.
>
> *Example 2:* Minister B is the minister of Church K. Church K publishes a monthly church newsletter that is distributed to all church members. In each issue, Minister B has a column titled "My Views." The month before the election, Minister B states in the "My Views" column, "It is my personal opinion that Candidate U should be reelected." For that one issue, Minister B pays from his personal funds the portion of the cost of the newsletter attributable to the "My Views" column. Even though he paid part of the cost of the newsletter, the newsletter is an official publication of the church. Since the endorsement appeared in an official publication of Church K, it constitutes campaign intervention attributed to Church K.
>
> *Example 3:* Minister C is the minister of Church L and is well known in the community. Three weeks before the election, he attends a press conference at Candidate V's campaign headquarters and states that Candidate V should be reelected. Minister C does not say he is speaking on behalf of his church. His endorsement is reported on the front page of the local newspaper and he is identified in the article as the minister of Church L. Since Minister C did not make the endorsement at an official church function, in an official church

publication, or otherwise use the church's assets, and did not state that he was speaking as a representative of Church L, his actions did not constitute campaign intervention attributable to Church L.

Example 4: Minister D is the minister of Church M. During regular services of Church M shortly before the election, Minister D preaches on a number of issues, including the importance of voting in the upcoming election, and concludes by stating, "It is important that you all do your duty in the election and vote for Candidate W." Since Minister D's remarks indicating support for Candidate W were made during an official church service, they constitute political campaign intervention attributable to Church M.

Inviting a Candidate to Speak

Depending on the facts and circumstances, a church or religious organization may invite political candidates to speak at its events without jeopardizing its tax-exempt status. Political candidates may be invited in their capacity as candidates, or individually (not as a candidate.)

Speaking as a candidate. Like any other IRC Section 501(C)(3) organization, when a candidate is invited to speak at a church or religious organization event as a political candidate, the church or religious organization must take steps to ensure that:

- It provides an equal opportunity to the political candidates seeking the same office,

- It does not indicate any support of or opposition to the candidate (this should be stated explicitly when the candidate is introduced and in communications concerning the candidate's attendance), and

- No political fund raising occurs.

Equal opportunity to participate. Like any other IRC Section 501(C)(3) organization, in determining whether candidates are given an equal opportunity to participate, a church or religious organization should consider the nature of the event to which each candidate is invited, in addition to the manner of presentation. For example, a church or religious organization that invites one candidate to speak at its well, attended annual banquet, but invites the opposing candidate to speak at a sparsely attended general meeting, will likely be found to have violated the political campaign prohibition, even if the manner of presentation for both speakers is otherwise neutral.

Public forum. Sometimes a church or religious organization invites several candidates to speak at a public forum. A public forum involving several candidates for public office may qualify as an exempt educational activity. However, if the forum is operated to show a bias for or against any candidate, then the forum would be prohibited campaign activity, as it would be considered intervention or participation in a political campaign. When an organization invites several candidates to speak at a forum, it should consider the following factors;

- Whether questions for the candidate are prepared and presented by an independent nonpartisan panel,

- Whether the topics discussed by the candidates cover a broad range of issues that the candidates would address if elected to the office sought and are of interest to the public,

- Whether each candidate is given an equal opportunity to present his or her views on the issues discussed,

- Whether the candidates are asked to agree or disagree with positions, agendas, platforms, or statements of the organization, and

- Whether a moderator comments on the questions or otherwise implies approval or disapproval of the candidates.

The following are two examples of situations where a church or religious organization invites a candidate to speak before the congregation.

> *Example 1: Minister E is the minister of Church N. In the month prior to the election, Minister E invited the three Congressional candidates for the district in which Church N is located to address the congregation, one each on three successive Sundays, as part of regular worship services. Each candidate was given an equal opportunity to address and field questions on a wide variety of topics from the congregation. Minister E's introduction of each candidate included no comments on their qualifications or any indication of a preference for any candidate. The actions do not constitute political campaign intervention by Church N.*

Example 2: Minister F is the minister of Church O. The Sunday before the November election, Minister F invited Senate Candidate X to preach to her congregation during worship services. During his remarks, Candidate X stated, "I am asking not only for your votes, but for your enthusiasm and dedication, for your willingness to go the extra mile to get a very large turnout on Tuesday." Minister F invited no other candidate to address her congregation during the senatorial campaign. Because these activities took place during official church services, they are attributed to Church O. By selectively providing church facilities to allow Candidate X to speak in support of his campaign, Church O's actions constitute political campaign intervention.

Speaking as a non-candidate. Like any other IRC Section 501(C)(3) organization, a church or religious organization may invite political candidates (including church members) to speak in a non-candidate capacity. For instance, a political candidate may be a public figure because he: (a) currently holds, or formerly held, public office; (b) is considered an expert in a non-political field; or (c) is a celebrity or has led a distinguished military, legal, or public service career. When a candidate is invited to speak at an event in a non-candidate capacity, it is not necessary for the church or religious organization to provide equal access to all political candidates. However, the church or religious organization must ensure that:

- The individual speaks only in a non-candidate capacity,

- Neither the individual nor any representative of the church makes any mention of his or her candidacy or the election, and

- No campaign activity occurs in connection with the candidate's attendance.

In addition, the church or religious organization should clearly indicate the capacity in which the candidate is appearing and should not mention the individual's political candidacy or the upcoming election in the communications announcing the candidate's attendance at the event. Below are examples of situations where a public official appears at a church or religious organization in an official capacity, and not as a candidate.

Example 1: Church P is located in the state capital. Minister G customarily acknowledges the presence of any public officials present during services. During the state gubernatorial race, Lieutenant Governor Y, a candidate, attended a

Wednesday evening prayer service in the church. Minister G acknowledged the Lieutenant Governor's presence in his customary manner, saying, "We are happy to have worshiping with us this evening Lieutenant Governor Y." Minister G made no reference in his welcome to the Lieutenant Governor's candidacy or the election. Minister G's actions do not constitute political campaign intervention by Church P.

Example 2: Minister H is the minister of Church Q. Church Q is building a community center. Minister H invites Congressman Z, the representative for the district containing Church Q, to attend the groundbreaking ceremony for the community center. Congressman Z is running for reelection at the time. Minister H makes no reference in her introduction to Congressman Z's candidacy or the election. Congressman Z also makes no reference to his candidacy or the election and does not do any fund raising while at Church Q. Church Q has not intervened in a political campaign.

Voter Guides

Like other IRC Section 501(C)(3) organizations, some churches and religious organizations undertake voter education activities by distributing voter guides. Voter guides, generally, are distributed during an election campaign and provide information on how all candidates stand on various issues. These guides may be distributed with the purpose of educating voters; however, they may not be used to attempt to favor or oppose candidates for public elected office. A careful review of the following facts and circumstances may help determine whether or not a church or religious organization's publication or distribution of voter guides constitutes prohibited political campaign activity:

- Whether the candidates' positions are compared to the organization's position,

- Whether the guide includes a broad range of issues that the candidates would address if elected to the office sought,

- Whether the description of issues is neutral,

- Whether all candidates for an office are included, and

- Whether the descriptions of candidates' positions are either:

- the candidates' own words in response to questions, or

- a neutral, unbiased, and complete compilation of all candidates' positions.

The following are examples of situations where churches distribute voter guides.

Example 1: Church R distributes a voter guide prior to elections. The voter guide consists of a brief statement from the candidates on each issue made in response to a questionnaire sent to all candidates for governor of State I. The issues on the questionnaire cover a wide variety of topics and were selected by Church R based solely on their importance and interest to the electorate as a whole. Neither the questionnaire nor the voter guide, through their content or structure, indicate a bias or preference for any candidate or group of candidates. Church R is not participating or intervening in a political campaign.

Example 2: Church S distributes a voter guide during an election campaign. The voter guide is prepared using the responses of candidates to a questionnaire sent to candidates for major public offices. Although the questionnaire covers a wide range of topics, the wording of the questions evidences a bias on certain issues. By using a questionnaire structured in this way, Church S is participating or intervening in a political campaign.

Business Activity

The question of whether an activity constitutes participation or intervention in a political campaign may also arise in the context of a business activity of the church or religious organization, such as the selling or renting of mailing lists, the leasing of office space, or the acceptance of paid political advertising. (The tax treatment of income from such unrelated business activities follows.) In this context, some of the factors to be considered in determining whether the church or religious organization has engaged in prohibited political campaign activity include the following:

- Whether the goods, services, or facility is available to the candidates on an equal basis,

- Whether the goods, services, or facility is available only to candidates and not to the general public,

- Whether the fees charged are at the organization's customary and usual rates, and

- Whether the activity is an ongoing activity of the organization or whether it is conducted only for the candidate.

Consequences of Political Campaign Activity

When it participates in political campaign activity, a church or religious organization jeopardizes both its tax-exempt status under IRC Section 501(C)(3) and its eligibility to receive tax-deductible contributions. In addition, it may become subject to an excise tax on its political expenditures. This *excise tax* may be imposed in addition to revocation, or it may be imposed instead of revocation. Also, the church or religious organization should correct the violation.

Excise tax. An initial tax is imposed on an organization at the rate of 10% of the political expenditures. Also, a tax at the rate of 2.5% of the expenditures is imposed against the organization managers (jointly and severally) who, without reasonable cause, agreed to the expenditures knowing they were political expenditures. The tax on management may not exceed $5,000 with respect to any one expenditure. In any case in which an initial tax is imposed against an organization, and the expenditures are not corrected within the period allowed by law, an additional tax equal to 100% of the expenditures is imposed against the organization. In that case, an additional tax is also imposed against the organization managers (jointly and severally) who refused to agree to make the correction. The additional tax on management is equal to 50% of the expenditures and may not exceed $10,000 with respect to any one expenditure.

Correction. Correction of a political expenditure requires the recovery of the expenditure, to the extent possible, and establishment of safeguards to prevent future political expenditures.

Please note that a church or religious organization that engages in any political campaign activity also needs to determine whether it is in compliance with the appropriate federal, state, or local election laws, as these may differ from the requirements under IRC Section 501(C)(3.)

UNRELATED BUSINESS INCOME TAX (UBIT)

Churches and religious organizations, like other tax-exempt organizations, may engage in income-producing activities unrelated to their tax-exempt purposes, as long as the unrelated activities are not a substantial part of the organization's activities. However, the net income from such activities will be subject to the UBIT if the following three conditions are met:

- The activity constitutes a trade or business,
- The trade or business is regularly carried on, and
- The trade or business is not substantially related to the organization's exempt purpose. (The fact that the organization uses the income to further its charitable or religious purposes does not make the activity substantially related to its exempt purposes.)

Exceptions to UBIT

Even if an activity meets the above three criteria, the income may not be subject to tax if it meets one of the following exceptions: (a) substantially all of the work in operating the trade or business is performed by volunteers; (b) the activity is conducted by the organization primarily for the convenience of its members; or (c) the trade or business involves the selling of merchandise substantially all of which was donated.

In general, rents from real property, royalties, capital gains, and interest and dividends are not subject to the unrelated business income tax unless financed with borrowed money.

Examples of Unrelated Trade or Business Activities

Unrelated trade or business activities vary depending on types of activities, as shown below.

Advertising

Many tax-exempt organizations sell advertising in their publications or other forms of public communication. Generally, income from the sale of advertising is unrelated trade or business income. This may include the sale of advertising space in weekly bulletins, magazines, or journals, or on church or religious organization Web sites.

Gaming

Most forms of gaming, if regularly carried on, may be considered the conduct of an unrelated trade or business. This can include the sale of pull-tabs and raffles. Income derived from bingo games may be eligible for a special tax exception (in addition to the exception regarding uncompensated volunteer labor covered above), if the following conditions are met: (a) the bingo game is the traditional type of bingo (as opposed to instant bingo, a variation of pull-tabs); (b) the conduct of the bingo game is not an activity carried out by for-profit organizations in the local area; and (c) the operation of the bingo game does not violate any state or local law.

Sale of Merchandise and Publications

The sale of merchandise and publications (including the actual publication of materials) can be considered the conduct of an unrelated trade or business if the items involved do not have a substantial relationship to the exempt purposes of the organization.

Rental Income

Generally, income derived from the rental of real property and incidental personal property is excluded from unrelated business income. However, there are certain situations in which rental income may be unrelated business taxable income:

- If a church rents out property on which there is debt outstanding (for example, a mortgage note), the rental income may constitute unrelated debt-financed income subject to UBIT. (However, if a church or convention or association of churches acquires debt-financed land for use in its exempt purposes within 15 years of the time of acquisition, then income from the rental of the land may not constitute unrelated business income.)

- If personal services are rendered in connection with the rental, then the income may be unrelated business taxable income, or

- If a church charges for the use of the parking lot, the income may be unrelated business taxable income.

Parking Lots

If a church owns a parking lot that is used by church members and visitors while attending church services, any parking fee paid to the church would not be subject to UBIT. However, if a church operates a parking lot that is used by members of the general public, parking fees would be taxable, as this activity would not be substantially related to the church's exempt purpose, and parking fees are not treated as rent from real property. If the church enters into a lease with a third party who operates the church's parking lot and pays rent to the church, such payments would not be subject to tax, as they would constitute rent from real property. Whether an income-producing activity is an unrelated trade or business activity depends on all the facts and circumstances. For more information, see IRS Publication 598, *Tax on Unrelated Business Income of Exempt Organizations*.

Tax on Income-Producing Activities

If a church, or other exempt organization, has gross income of $1,000 or more for any taxable year from the conduct of any unrelated trade or business, it is required to file IRS Form 990-T, *Exempt Organization Business Income Tax Return*, for that year. If the church is part of a larger entity (such as a diocese), it must file a separate Form 990-T if it has a separate EIN. Form 990-T is due the 15th day of the fifth month following the end of the church's tax year. (IRC Section 512(b)(12) provides a special rule for parishes and similar local units of a church. A specific deduction is provided, which is equal to the lower of $1,000 or the gross income derived from any unrelated trade or business regularly carried on by such parish or local unit of a church.) See Filing Requirements on page 163.

EMPLOYMENT TAX

Generally, churches and religious organizations are required to withhold, report, and pay over-withheld income and Federal Insurance Contributions Act (FICA) taxes for their employees. Employment tax includes income tax withheld and paid for an employee and FICA taxes withheld and paid on behalf of an employee. Substantial penalties may be imposed against an organization that fails to withhold and pay the proper employment tax. Whether a church or religious organization must withhold and pay employment tax depends upon whether the church's workers are employees. *Determination of worker status* is important. Several facts determine whether a worker is an employee. For an in-depth explanation and examples of the common law employer-employee relationship, see IRS Publication 15-A, *Employer's Supplemental Tax Guide*. If a church or a worker wants the IRS to determine whether the worker is an employee, the church or worker should file IRS Form SS-8, *Determination of Employee Worker Status for Purposes of Federal Employment Taxes and Income Tax Withholding*, with the IRS.

Social Security and Medicare Taxes — Federal Insurance Contributions Act (FICA)

FICA taxes consist of Social Security and Medicare taxes. Wages paid to employees of churches or religious organizations are subject to FICA taxes unless *one* of the following exceptions applies:

- Wages are paid for services performed by a duly ordained, commissioned, or licensed minister of a church in the exercise of his or her ministry, or by a member of a religious order in the exercise of duties required by such order,

- The church or religious organization pays the employee wages of less than $108.28 in a calendar year, or

- A church that is opposed to the payment of Social Security and Medicare taxes for religious reasons files IRS Form 8274, *Certification by Churches and Qualified Church Controlled Organizations Electing Exemption From Employer Social Security and Medicare Taxes.*

  Very specific timing rules apply to filing Form 8274. It must be filed before the first date on which the electing entity is required to file its first quarterly employment tax return. This election does not relieve the organization of its obligation to withhold income tax on wages paid to its employees. In addition, if such an election is made, affected employees must pay Self-Employment Contributions Act (SECA) tax. For further information, see Publication 517, *Social Security and Other Information for Members of the Clergy and Religious Workers.*

Withheld employee income tax and FICA taxes are reported on IRS Form 941, *Employer's Quarterly Federal Tax Return.* For more information about employment tax, see IRS Publication 15, *Circular E, Employer's Tax Guide*, and IRS Publication 15-A, *Employer's Supplemental Tax Guide.* See also, IRS Publication 517, *Social Security and Other Information for Members of the Clergy and Religious Workers.*

Federal Unemployment Tax Act (FUTA)

Churches and religious organizations are not liable for FUTA tax. For further information on FUTA, see IRS Publication 517, *Social Security and Other Information for Members of the*

Clergy and Religious Workers.

SPECIAL RULES FOR COMPENSATION OF MINISTERS

Withholding Income Tax for Ministers

Unlike other exempt organizations or businesses, a church is not required to withhold income tax from the compensation that it pays to its duly ordained, commissioned, or licensed ministers for performing services in the exercise of their ministry. An employee minister may, however, enter into a voluntary withholding agreement with the church by completing IRS Form W-4, *Employee's Withholding Allowance Certificate*. A church should report compensation paid to a minister on Form W-2, *Wage and Tax Statement*, if the minister is an employee, or on IRS Form 1099-MISC, *Miscellaneous Income*, if the minister is an independent contractor.

Parsonage or Housing Allowances

Generally, a minister's gross income does not include the fair rental value of a home (parsonage) provided, or a housing allowance paid, as part of the minister's compensation for services performed that are ordinarily the duties of a minister.

A minister who is furnished a *parsonage* may exclude from income the fair rental value of the parsonage, including utilities. However, the amount excluded cannot be more than the reasonable pay for the minister's services.

A minister who receives a *housing allowance* may exclude the allowance from gross income to the extent it is used to pay expenses in providing a home. Generally, those expenses include rent, mortgage payments, utilities, repairs, and other expenses directly relating to providing a home. If a minister owns a home, the amount excluded from the minister's gross income as a housing allowance is limited to the least of the following: (a) the amount actually used to provide a home; (b) the amount officially designated as a housing allowance; or (c) the fair rental value of the home. The minister's church or other qualified organization must designate the housing allowance pursuant to official action taken in advance of the payment. If a minister is employed and paid by a local congregation, a designation by a national church agency will not be effective. The local congregation must make the designation. A national church agency may make an effective designation for ministers it directly employs. If none of the minister's salary has been officially designated as a housing allowance, the full salary must be included in gross income.

The fair rental value of a parsonage or housing allowance is excludable from income only for income tax purposes. These amounts are *not* excluded in determining the minister's net earnings from self-employment for Self-Employment Contributions Act (SECA) tax purposes. Retired ministers who receive either a parsonage or housing allowance are not required to include such amounts for SECA tax purposes.

A minister who owns or is purchasing a home may exclude the parsonage allowance from gross income to the extent it is used for the down payment, mortgage payments, interest, real estate taxes, utilities, and repairs.

As mentioned above, a minister who receives a parsonage or rental allowance excludes that amount from his income. The portion of expenses allocable to the excludable amount is not deductible. This limitation, however, does not apply to interest on a home mortgage or real estate taxes, nor to the calculation of net earnings from self-employment for SECA tax purposes.

IRS Publication 517, *Social Security and Other Information for Members of the Clergy and Religious Workers*, has a detailed example of the tax treatment for a housing allowance and the related limitations on deductions. IRS Publication 525, *Taxable and Nontaxable Income*, has information on particular types of income for ministers.

Reimbursement for Automobile Expenses

Probably the most common business expense that a church may be reimbursing for its automobile business mileage. Generally, the amount of a mileage allowance that a church pays at a rate that is less than or equal to the federal standard rate is treated as being substantiated and is treated as paid under an accountable plan with no employment tax consequences to the reimbursed individual, providing that the employee documents the time, place, and business purpose of the reimbursement. Each year, the federal government establishes a standard mileage reimbursement rate.

Social Security and Medicare Taxes – Federal Insurance Contributions Act (FICA) vs. Self-Employment Contributions Act (SECA)

The compensation that a church or religious organization pays to its ministers for performing services in the exercise of ministry is not subject to FICA taxes. However, income that a minister earns in performing services in the exercise of his ministry is subject to SECA tax, unless the minister has timely applied for and received an exemption from SECA tax.

PAYMENT OF EMPLOYEES, BUSINESS EXPENSES

A church or religious organization is treated like any other employer with regard to the tax rules regarding employee business expenses. The rules differ depending upon whether the expenses are paid through an accountable or non-accountable plan, and these plans determine whether the payment for these expenses is included in the employee's income.

Accountable Reimbursement Plan

An arrangement that an employer establishes to reimburse or advance employee business expenses will be an accountable plan if it meets three requirements: (1) involves a business connection; (2) requires the employee to substantiate expenses incurred; and (3) requires the employee to return any excess amounts.

Employees must provide the organization with sufficient information to identify the specific business nature of each expense and to substantiate each element of an expenditure. It is not sufficient for an employee to aggregate expenses into broad categories such as travel or to report expenses through the use of non-descriptive terms such as *miscellaneous business expenses*. Both the substantiation and the return of excess amounts must occur within a reasonable period of time.

Employee business expenses reimbursed under an accountable plan are (a) excluded from an employee's gross income; (b) not required to be reported on the employee's IRS Form W-2, *Wage and Tax Statement*; and (c) exempt from the withholding and payment of wages subject to FICA taxes and income tax withholdings.

Non-accountable Reimbursement Plan

If the church or religious organization reimburses or advances the employee for business expenses, but the arrangement does not satisfy the three requirements of an accountable plan, the amounts paid to the employees are considered wages subject to FICA taxes and income tax withholding, if applicable, and are reportable on Form W-2. (Amounts paid to employee ministers are treated as wages reportable on Form W-2, but are not subject to FICA taxes or income tax withholding.)

For example, if a church or religious organization pays its secretary a $200-per-month allowance to reimburse monthly business expenses the secretary incurs while conducting church or religious organization business, and the secretary is not required to substantiate the expenses or return any excess, then the entire $200 must be reported on Form W-2 as wages subject to FICA taxes and income tax withholding. In the same situation involving an employee-minister, the allowance must be reported on the minister's Form W-2, but no FICA or income tax withholding is required. For further information, see IRS Publication 463, *Travel, Entertainment, Gift and Car Expenses.*

One common business expense reimbursement is for *automobile mileage.* If a church or religious organization pays a mileage allowance at a rate that is less than or equal to the federal standard rate, the amount of the expense is deemed substantiated. (Each year, the federal government establishes a standard mileage reimbursement rate.) There are no income or employment tax consequences to the reimbursed individual provided that the employee substantiates the time, place, and business purposes of the automobile mileage for which reimbursement is sought. Of course, reimbursement for automobile mileage incurred for personal purposes is includible in the individual's income.

If a church or religious organization reimburses automobile mileage at a rate exceeding the standard mileage rate, the excess is treated as paid under a non-accountable plan. This means that the excess is includible in the individual's income and is subject to the withholding and payment of income and employment taxes, if applicable. In addition, any mileage reimbursement that is paid without requiring the individual to substantiate the time, place, and business purposes of each trip is included in the individual's income, regardless of the rate of reimbursement.

No income is attributed to an employee or a volunteer who uses an automobile owned by the church or religious organization to perform church-related work.

RECORD KEEPING REQUIREMENTS

Books of Accounting and Other Types of Records

All tax-exempt organizations, including churches and religious organizations (regardless of whether tax-exempt status has been officially recognized by the IRS), are required to maintain books of accounting and other records necessary to justify their claim for exemption in the event of an audit. See Special Rules Limiting IRS Authority to Audit a Church on page 168. Tax-exempt organizations are also required to maintain books and records that are necessary to accurately file any federal tax and information returns that may be required.

There is no specific format for keeping records. However, the types of required records frequently include organizing documents (charter, constitution, articles of incorporation) and bylaws, minute books, property records, general ledgers, receipts and disbursements journals, payroll records, banking records, and invoices. The extent of the records necessary generally varies according to the type, size, and complexity of the organization's activities.

Length of Time to Retain Records

The law does not specify a *length of time* that records must be retained; however, the following guidelines should be applied in the event that the records may be material to the administration of any federal tax law.

Type of Record and Length of Time to Retain

Type - Records of revenue and expenses including payroll records.

Length of Time - Retain for at least four and expenses, years after filing the return(s) to which they relate.

Type - Records relating to acquisition and disposition of property (real and personal, including investments)

Length of Time - Retain for at least four years after the filing of the return for the year in which disposition occurs.

FILING REQUIREMENTS

Churches or religious organizations may be required to report certain payments to the IRS. The following is a list of the most frequently required returns, who should use them, how they are used, and when they should be filed.

<u>Form W-2 Wage and Tax Statement</u>

Furnish each employee with a completed Form W-2 by January 31st; and file all Forms W-2 and Form W-3 with the Social Security Administration (SSA) by the last day of February.

<u>Form W-3</u>

Transmittal of Wage and Tax Statement Form W-2G

Certain Gaming Winnings

Any charitable or religious organization, including a church, that sponsors a gaming event (raffles, bingo) must file Form W-2G when a participant wins a prize over a specific value amount. For each winner meeting the filing requirement, the church or religious organization must furnish each winner Form W-2G by January 31st; and file Copy A of Form W-2G with the IRS by February 28th. The requirements for reporting and withholding depend on the type of gaming, the amount of winnings, and the ratio of winnings to the wager. For more information on reporting requirements for gaming activities, see IRS Publication 3079, *Gaming Publication for Tax-Exempt Organizations.*

Form 941

Employer's Quarterly Federal Tax Return

Use Form 941 to report Social Security and Medicare taxes and income taxes withheld by the organization, and Social Security and Medicare taxes paid by the organization. The returns are due on April 30th, July 31st, October 31st, and January 31st (10 days later if the organization deposited all taxes when due.)

Form 945

Annual Return of Withheld Federal Income Tax

If a church or religious organization withholds income tax, including backup withholding, from non-payroll payments, it must file Form 945. File Form 945 by January 31st. This form is not required for those years in which there is no non-payroll tax liability.

Form 990

Return of Organization Exempt from Income Tax

Generally, all religious organizations (see Exceptions to file 990 below) must file Form 990 or Form 990-EZ unless their annual gross receipts do not normally exceed $25,000. Form 990-EZ is a simplified version of Form 990 that can be used by organizations that have annual gross receipts of less than $100,000 and have total assets of less than $250,000 at the end of the year. Generally, Form 990 or Form 990-EZ must be filed on or before the 15th day of the fifth month following the end of the organization's annual accounting period (May 15 for a calendar year accounting period.) The organization must include Schedule A (Form 990 or Form 990-EZ) when it files. Schedule B (Form 990 or Form 990-EZ) may also be required.

Exceptions to file 990

The following is a list of some of the organizations that are not required to file Form 990.

- churches (as opposed to "religious organizations," defined earlier)
- inter-church organizations of local units of a church
- mission societies sponsored by or affiliated with one or more churches or church denominations, if more than half of the activities are conducted in, or directed at, persons in foreign countries
- an exclusively religious activity of any religious order

For a list of other organizations that are not required to file Form 990, see the Instructions for Form 990 and Form 990-EZ.

Form 990-T

Exempt Organization Business Income Tax Return

Churches and religious organizations must file Form 990-T if they generate gross income from an unrelated business of $1,000 or more for a taxable year. For more information on unrelated business income, see Unrelated Business Income Tax (UBIT) on page 153. Form 990-T must be filed by the 15th day of the fifth month after the organization's accounting period ends (May 15th for a calendar year accounting period.)

Form 990-W

Estimated Tax on Unrelated Business Taxable Income for Tax-Exempt Organizations

If the tax on unrelated business income is expected to be $500 or more, the church or religious organization must make estimated tax payments. Use Form 990-W to compute the estimated tax liability.

Form 1096

Annual Summary and Transmittal of U.S. Information Returns

Churches and religious organizations. Use Form 1096 to transmit Forms 1099-MISC, W-2G, and certain other forms to the IRS. Form 1096 must be filed by February 28th in the year following the calendar year in which the payments were made. *Churches and religious organizations.*

Form 1099

Miscellaneous Income

A church or religious organization must use Form 1099-MISC if it pays an unincorporated individual or an entity $600 or more in any calendar year for one of the following payments:

(a) gross rents

(b) commissions

(c) fees, or other compensation paid to non-employees

(d) prizes and awards

(e) other fixed and determinable income

Churches or religious organizations must furnish each payee with a copy of Form 1099-MISC by January 31st; and file Copy A of Form 1099-MISC with the IRS by February 28th.

Form 5578

Annual Certification of Racial Nondiscrimination for a Private School Exempt from Federal Income Tax

A church or religious organization that operates a private school, whether separately incorporated or operated as part of its overall operations, that teaches secular subjects and generally complies with state law requirements for public education. Form 5578 must be filed on or before the 15th day of the fifth month following the end of the organization's taxable year (May 15 for a calendar year.) If an organization files Form 990 or Form 990-EZ, the certification must be made on Schedule A (Form 990 or Form 990-EZ.)

Note: It is not considered racially discriminatory for a parochial school to select students on the basis of membership in a religious denomination if membership in the denomination is open to all on a racially nondiscriminatory basis. Further, a seminary, or other purely religious school, that primarily teaches religious subjects usually with the purpose of training students for the ministry, is not subject to the racially nondiscriminatory requirements because it is considered to be a religious rather than an educational organization. The church or religious organization must file Form 8282 with the IRS within 125 days of date of disposition of the property; and furnish the original donor with a copy of the form.

A church or religious organization must file Form 5578 to certify that it does not discriminate based on race or ethnic origin. For information on racial and ethnic nondiscriminatory policies, see Revenue Procedure 75-50, 1975-2 C.B. 587 at www.irs.gov.

Form 8282

Donee Information Return

A church or religious organization must file Form 8282 if it sells, exchanges, transfers, or otherwise disposes of certain non-cash donated property within two years of the date it originally received the donation. This applies to non-cash property that had an appraised value of $5,000 or more at time of donation. This donee must also furnish a copy of the form to the original donor.

CHARITABLE CONTRIBUTIONS - SUBSTANTIATION AND DISCLOSURE RULES

There are two general rules that a church or religious organization needs to be aware of to meet substantiation and disclosure requirements for federal income tax return reporting purposes.

- A donor is responsible for obtaining a written acknowledgment from a charity for any single contribution of $250 or more before the donor can claim a charitable contribution on his or her federal income tax return.

- A charitable organization is required to provide a written disclosure to a donor who receives goods or services in exchange for a single payment in excess of $75.

Substantiation Rules

A donor cannot claim a tax deduction for any single contribution of $250 or more unless the donor obtains a contemporaneous, written acknowledgment of the contribution from the recipient church or religious organization. A church or religious organization that does not acknowledge a contribution incurs no penalty; but without a written acknowledgment, the donor cannot claim a tax deduction. Although it is a donor's responsibility to obtain a written acknowledgment, a church or religious organization can assist the donor by providing a timely, written statement containing the following information:

- Name of the church or religious organization,

- Date of the contribution,

- Amount of any cash contribution, and

- Description (but not the value) of non-cash contributions.

In addition, the timely, written statement must contain one of the following:

- Statement that no goods or services were provided by the church or religious organization in return for the contribution,

- Statement that goods or services that a church or religious organization provided in return for the contribution consisted entirely of intangible religious benefits, or

- Description and good faith estimate of the value of goods or services other than intangible religious benefits that the church or religious organization provided in return for the contribution.

The church or religious organization may either provide separate acknowledgments for each single contribution of $250 or more or one acknowledgment to substantiate several single contributions of $250 or more. Separate contributions are not aggregated for purposes of measuring the $250 threshold.

Disclosure Rules that Apply to *Quid Pro Quo* Contributions

A contribution made by a donor in exchange for goods or services is known as a *quid pro quo* contribution. A donor may only take a contribution deduction to the extent that his or her contribution exceeds the fair market value of the goods and services the donor receives in return for the contribution. Therefore, donors need to know the value of the goods or services. A church or religious organization must provide a written statement to a donor who makes a payment exceeding $75 partly as a contribution and partly for goods and services provided by the organization.

Example 1: If a donor gives a church a payment of $100 and, in return, receives a ticket to an event valued at $40, this is a quid pro quo *contribution, and only $60 is deductible by the donor ($100 - $40 = $60.) Even though the deductible amount does not exceed $75, since the* quid pro quo *contribution the church received is in excess of $75, the church must provide the donor with a written disclosure statement. The statement must: (1) inform the donor that the amount of the contribution that is deductible for federal income tax purposes is limited to the excess of money (and the fair market value of any property other than money)* *contributed by the donor over the value of goods or services provided by the church or religious organization; and (2) provide the donor with a good-faith estimate of the value of the goods or services.*

The church or religious organization must provide the written disclosure statement with either the solicitation or the receipt of the contribution and in a manner that is likely to come to the attention of the donor. For example, a disclosure in small print within a larger document may not meet this requirement.

Exceptions to Disclosure Statement

A church or religious organization is not required to provide a disclosure statement for *quid pro quo* contributions when: (a) the goods or services meet the standards for *insubstantial value*; or (b) the only benefit received by the donor is an *intangible religious benefit*. Additionally, if the goods or services the church or religious organization provides are *intangible religious benefits* (examples follow), the acknowledgment for contributions of $250 or more does not need to describe those benefits.

Generally, intangible religious benefits are benefits provided by a church or religious organization that are not usually sold in commercial transactions outside a donative (gift) context.

Intangible religious benefits include:

- Admission to a religious ceremony

- *De minimus* tangible benefits, such as wine used in a religious ceremony

Benefits that are not intangible religious benefits include:

- Tuition for education leading to a recognized degree

- Travel services

- Consumer goods

IRS Publication 1771, Charitable Contributions: Substantiation and Disclosure Requirements, *provides more information on substantiation and disclosure rules. Order Publication 1771 free through the IRS at (800) 829-3676.*

SPECIAL RULES LIMITING IRS AUTHORITY TO AUDIT A CHURCH

Tax Inquiries and Examinations of Churches

Congress has imposed special limitations, found in IRC Section 7611, on how and when the IRS may conduct civil tax inquiries and examinations of churches. The IRS may only initiate a church tax inquiry if the Director, Exempt Organizations, Examinations reasonably believes, based on a written statement of the facts and circumstances, that the organization (a) may not qualify for the exemption; or (b) may not be paying tax on an unrelated business or other taxable activity.

Restrictions on Church Inquiries and Examinations

Restrictions on church inquiries and examinations apply only to churches (including organizations claiming to be churches if such status has not been recognized by IRS) and conventions or associations of churches. They do not apply to related persons or organizations. Thus, for example, the rules do not apply to schools that, although operated by a church, are organized as separate legal entities. Similarly, the rules do not apply to integrated auxiliaries of a church.

Restrictions on church inquiries and examinations do not apply to all church inquiries by the IRS. The most common exception relates to routine requests for information. For example, IRS requests for information from churches about filing of returns, compliance with income or Social Security and Medicare tax withholding requirements, supplemental information needed to process returns or applications, and other similar inquiries are not covered by the special church audit rules.

Restrictions on church inquiries and examinations do not apply to criminal investigations or to investigations of the tax liability of any person connected with the church; e.g., a contributor or minister. The procedures of IRC Section 7611 will be used in initiating and conducting any inquiry or examination into whether an excess benefit transaction (as that term is used in IRC Section 4958) has occurred between a church and an insider.

Audit Process

The following is the sequence of the audit process.

1. If the *reasonable belief* requirement is met, the IRS must begin an inquiry by providing a church with written notice containing an explanation of its concerns.

2. The church is allowed a reasonable period in which to respond by furnishing a written explanation to alleviate IRS concerns.

3. If the church fails to respond within the required time, or if its response is not sufficient to alleviate IRS concerns, the IRS may, generally within 90 days, issue a second notice, informing the church of the need to examine its books and records.

4. After issuance of a second notice, but before commencement of an examination of its books and records, the church may request a conference with an IRS official to discuss IRS concerns. The second notice will contain a copy of all documents collected or prepared by the IRS for use in the examination and subject to disclosure under the Freedom of Information Act, as supplemented by IRC Section 6103 relating to disclosure and confidentiality of tax return information.

5. Generally, examination of a church's books and records must be completed within two years from the date of the second notice from the IRS.

If at any time during the inquiry process the church supplies information sufficient to alleviate the concerns of the IRS, the matter will be closed without examination of the church's books and records. There are additional safeguards for the protection of churches under IRC Section 7611. For example, the IRS cannot begin a subsequent examination of a church for a five-year period unless the previous examination resulted in a revocation, notice of deficiency of assessment, or a request for a significant change in church operations, including a significant change in accounting practices.

GLOSSARY OF TERMS

Church. Certain characteristics are generally attributed to churches. These attributes of a church have been developed by the IRS and by court decisions. They include distinct legal existence; recognized creed and form of worship; definite and distinct ecclesiastical government; formal code of doctrine and discipline; distinct religious history; membership not associated with any other church or denomination; organization of ordained ministers;

ordained ministers selected after completing prescribed courses of study; literature of its own; established places of worship; regular congregations; regular religious services; Sunday schools for the religious instruction of the young; schools for the preparation of its ministers.

The IRS generally uses a combination of these characteristics, together with other facts and circumstances, to determine whether an organization is considered a church for federal tax purposes. The IRS makes no attempt to evaluate the content of whatever doctrine a particular organization claims is religious, provided the particular beliefs of the organization are truly and sincerely held by those professing them and the practices and rites associated with the organization's belief or creed are not illegal or contrary to clearly defined public policy.

Integrated Auxiliary of a Church. The term *integrated auxiliary of a church* refers to a class of organizations that are related to a church or convention or association of churches, but are not such organizations themselves. In general, the IRS will treat an organization that meets the following three requirements as an integrated auxiliary of a church. The organization must:

- be described both as an IRC Section 501(C)(3) charitable organization and as a public charity under IRC Sections 509(a)(1), (2), or (3),

- be affiliated with a church or convention or association of churches, and

- receive financial support primarily from internal church sources as opposed to public or governmental sources.

Men's and women's organizations, seminaries, mission societies, and youth groups that satisfy the first two requirements above are considered integrated auxiliaries whether or not they meet the internal support requirements. More guidance as to the types of organizations the IRS will treat as integrated auxiliaries can be found in the Code of Regulations, 26 CFR Section 1.6033-2(h.)

The same rules that apply to a church apply to the integrated auxiliary of a church, with the exception of those rules that apply to the audit of a church. See Special Rules Limiting IRS Authority to Audit a Church on page 168.

Minister. The term minister is not used by all faiths; however, in an attempt to make this publication easy to read, we use it because it is generally understood. As used in this booklet, the term minister denotes members of clergy of all religions and denominations and includes priests, rabbis, imams, and similar members of the clergy.

IRC Section 501(C)(3). IRC Section 501(C)(3) describes charitable organizations, including churches and religious organizations, which qualify for exemption from federal income tax and generally are eligible to receive tax-deductible contributions. This section provides that:

- an organization must be organized and operated exclusively for religious or other charitable purposes,

- net earnings may not inure to the benefit of any private individual or shareholder,

- no substantial part of its activity may be attempting to influence legislation,

- the organization may not intervene in political campaigns, and

- the organization's purposes and activities may not be illegal or violate fundamental public policy.

These requirements are set forth in greater detail throughout this publication.

HELP FROM THE IRS

Publication 1 *Your Rights as a Taxpayer*

Publication 15 Circular E, *Employer's Tax Guide*

Publication 15-A *Employer's Supplemental Tax Guide*

Publication 334 *Tax Guide for Small Business (For Individuals Who Use Schedule C or C-EZ)*

Publication 463 *Travel, Entertainment, Gift, and Car Expenses*

Publication 517 *Social Security and Other Information for Members of the Clergy and Religious Workers*

Publication 525 *Taxable and Nontaxable Income*

Publication 526 *Charitable Contributions*

Publication 557 *Tax-Exempt Status for Your Organization*

Publication 561 *Determining the Value of Donated Property*

Publication 571 *Tax-Sheltered Annuity Programs for Employees of Public Schools and Certain Tax-Exempt Organizations*

Publication 598 *Tax on Unrelated Business Income of Exempt Organizations*

Publication 910 *Guide to Free Tax Services*

Publication 1771 *Charitable Contributions: Substantiation and Disclosure*

Publication 3079 *Gaming Publication for Tax-Exempt Organizations*

Tax Publications for Exempt Organizations

Get publications via the Internet and free through the IRS at (800) 829-3676:

Pub 517, *Social Security and Other Information for Members of the Clergy and Religious Workers*

Pub 526, *Charitable Contributions*

Pub 557, *Tax-Exempt Status for Your Organization*

Pub 578, *Tax Information for Private Foundations and Foundation Managers*

Pub 598, *Tax on Unrelated Business Income of Exempt Organizations*

Pub 1771, *Charitable Contributions— Substantiation and Disclosure Requirements*

Pub 1828, *Tax Guide for Churches and Religious Organizations*

Pub 3079, *Gaming Publication for Tax-Exempt Organizations*

Pub 3833, *Disaster Relief, Providing Assistance through Charitable Organizations*

Forms for Exempt Organizations

Form SS-4, *Application for Employer Identification Number*

Form 990, *Return of Organization Exempt From Income Tax*

Form 990-EZ, *Short Form Return of Organization Exempt From Income Tax*

Form 990-PF, *Return of Private Foundation or Section 4947(a)(1) Nonexempt Charitable Trust Treated as a Private Foundation* Schedule A, of Form 990 or 990-EZ, *Supplementary Information – Organization Exempt Under Section 501(C)(3)*, Schedule B, of Form 990, 990-EZ, or 990-PF, *Schedule of Contributors*

Form 990-T, *Exempt Organization Business Income Tax Return,* (and proxy tax under section 6033(e))

Form 990-W, *Estimated Tax on Unrelated Business Taxable Income for Exempt Organizations* (and on Investment Income for Private Foundations)

Form 1023, *Application for Recognition of Exemption Under Section 501(C)(3) of the Internal Revenue Code*

Form 2848, *Power of Attorney and Declaration of Representative*

Form 8821, *Tax Information Authorization*

APPENDIX

This section contains Bylaws for Individuals, and Bylaws for Religious Ministries.

THE BEST GUIDE FOR NONPROFIT CORPORATIONS

SAMPLE NON-RELIGIOUS CORPORATION BYLAWS

BYLAWS OF

_____

(your corporation name here)

A Nonprofit Corporation

ARTICLE I

INTRODUCTION

Definition of Bylaws

1.01 These Bylaws constitute the code of rule adopted by _____ for the regulation and management of its affairs.

Purposes and Powers

1.02 This Corporation will have the purposes or powers as stated in its Articles of Incorporation, and whatever powers are or may be granted by the Nonprofit Corporation Law or any successor legislation.

The primary purpose of this Corporation is for educational, therapeutic and charitable purposes, more specifically, to provide (insert your purpose)_____.

ARTICLE II

OFFICES AND AGENCY

Principal and Branch Offices

2.01 The principal place of business of this Corporation is (city, state)_____. In addition, the Corporation may maintain other offices either within or outside the State of Florida.

Location of Registered Office

2.02 The location of the registered office of this Corporation is stated in the Articles of Incorporation. This office will be continuously maintained in the duration of the Corporation. The Board of Directors may from time to time change the address of its registered office by duly adopted resolution and amend its Articles of Incorporation and file the appropriate statement with the Department of State.

ARTICLE III

MEMBERSHIP

3.01 The Corporation shall not have members. The authority to carry on the business of the Corporation shall vest in the Board of Directors.

ARTICLE IV

DIRECTORS

Definition of Board of Directors

4.01 The Board of Directors is that group of persons vested with the management of the business and affairs of this Corporation.

Structure of Board

4.02 The Board of Directors of this Corporation will constitute a single class.

Qualifications of Directors

4.03 The qualifications for becoming and remaining a Director of this Corporation are as follows:

(1) Directors must be age eighteen (18) years of age or older.

Number of Directors

4.04 The number of Directors of this Corporation will not be fewer than three (3) at any time. Until further amendment of these Bylaws, the number of Directors presently will be seven (7.)

Terms of Directors

4.05　The Directors constituting the first Board of Directors as named in the Articles of Incorporation will hold office until February 28, 2004. Thereafter, Directors will be elected for a term of three (3) years. Each Director will hold office for the term for which elected and until a successor has been selected and qualified. At the last meeting of the Board of Directors in each three- (3) year term, a slate of Directors shall be nominated by the President and elected by a majority vote (with each Director to receive a majority vote, individually) of the Directors present at said meeting. Directors may serve an unlimited number of consecutive terms.

Vacancies on the Board

4.06　Any vacancy occurring on the Board of Directors, and any directorship to be filled by reason of an increase in the number of Directors, will be filled by election by a majority of the remaining Board of Directors at a special meeting to be called by the President. The new Director elected to fill the vacancy will serve for the unexpired term of the predecessor in office.

Location of Directors' Meetings

4.07　Meetings of the Board of Directors, regular and special, will be held at _____ or such places as the Board of Directors designates by resolution duly adopted or as the President specially designates.

Location of Directors' Meetings

4.08　Regular meetings of the Board of Directors will be held on the first Monday of the first month of each calendar quarter. If the date set for the meeting falls on a legal business holiday, then the meeting will be held on the following Monday instead. This provision of the bylaws constitutes notice to all Directors of all regular meetings, and no further notice shall be required, although further notice may be given.

Notice of Special Directors' Meetings

4.09 Written or printed notice stating the place, day, and hours of any special meeting of the Board of Directors will be delivered to each Director not less than two (2) nor more than twenty-one (21) days before the date of the meeting, either personally or by first class mail, by or at the direction of the President, or the Secretary, or the Directors calling the meeting. If mailed, the notice will be deemed to be delivered when deposited in the United States mail addressed to the Director at his address as it appears on the records of this Corporation, with postage prepaid. The notice need not state the business to be transacted at, nor the purpose of, the meeting.

Call of Special Board Meetings

4.10 A special meeting of the Board of Directors may be called by either:

(1) The President

(2) A majority of the Board of Directors

Waiver of Notice

4.11 Attendance of a Director at any meeting of the Board of Directors will constitute a waiver of notice of that meeting except when the Director attends a meeting for the express purpose of objecting, at the beginning of the meeting, to the transaction of any business because the meeting is not lawfully called or convened.

Quorum of Directors

4.12 A majority of the whole Board of Directors will constitute a quorum. The act of majority of the Directors present at a meeting at which a quorum is present will be the act of the Board of Directors unless a greater number is required under the provision of the Nonprofit Corporation Law of 1972, the Articles of Incorporation of this Corporation, or any provision of these Bylaws.

Removal of Directors

4.13 Any director may be removed by a majority vote of the Board of Directors.

ARTICLE V

OFFICERS

Roster of Officers

5.01 The Officers of this Corporation will consist of the following personnel:

(1) President

(2) Vice President

(3) Secretary

(4) Treasurer

Selection of Officers

5.02 Each of the Officers of this Corporation will be elected and appointed annually by the Board of Directors. Each Officer will remain in office until a successor to the office has been selected and qualified. Elections will be held at the regular meeting of the Board of Directors taking place at the first meeting of the calendar year.

Multiple Officeholders

5.03 In any election of Officers, the Board of Directors may elect and appoint a single person to more than one office simultaneously, except that the offices of President and Secretary, and President and Treasurer must be held by separate individuals.

President

5.04 The President is the Chief Executive Officer of this Corporation and will, subject to the control of the Board of Directors or any Committees, supervise and control the affairs of the Corporation. The President will perform all duties incident to the office and any other duties that may be required by these Bylaws or prescribed by the Board of Directors.

Vice President

5.05 The Vice President will perform all duties and exercise all powers of the President when the President is absent or is otherwise unable to act. The Vice President will perform any other duties that may be prescribed by the Board of Directors.

Secretary

5.06 The Secretary will keep minutes of all meetings of Members and of the Board of Directors, be the custodian of the corporate records, give all notices as are required by law or by these Bylaws, and generally perform all duties incident to the office of Secretary and any other duties as may be required by law, by the Articles of Incorporation, or by these Bylaws, or which may be assigned by the Board of Directors.

Treasurer

5.07 The treasurer will have charge and custody of all funds of this Corporation, and will deposit the funds as required by the Board of Directors, keep and maintain adequate and correct accounts of the Corporation's properties and business transactions, and render reports and accountings to the Directors. The Treasurer will perform in general all duties incident to the office of Treasurer and any other duties as may be required by law, by the Articles of Incorporation, or by these Bylaws, or which may be assigned by the Board of Directors.

Removal of Officers

5.08 Any Officer elected or appointed to office may be removed by the persons authorized under these Bylaws to elect or appoint Officers whenever in their judgment the best interests of this Corporation will be served. However, any removal will be without prejudice to any contract rights of the Officer so removed.

ARTICLE VI

INFORMAL ACTION

Waiver of Notice

6.01 Whenever any notice whatever is required to be given under the provisions of the Nonprofit Corporation Law of 1972, the Articles of Incorporation of this Corporation, or these Bylaws, a waiver of the notice, in writing signed by the person or persons entitled to notice, whether before of after the time stated in the waiver, will be deemed equivalent to the giving of the notice. The waiver must, in the case of a special meeting of Members, specify the general nature of the business to be transacted.

Action by Consent

6.02 Any action required by law or under the Articles of Incorporation of this Corporation or these Bylaws, or any action which otherwise may be taken at a meeting of either the Members or Board of Directors, may be taken without a meeting if a consent in writing, setting forth the action taken, is signed by all the persons entitled to vote with respect to the subject matter of the consent, or all Directors in office, and filed with the Secretary of the Corporation.

ARTICLE VII

COMMITTEES

Functionary Committees

7.01 The Board of Directors, by resolution, may designate and appoint certain Functionary Committees designated to transact certain ministerial business of the Corporation or to advise the Board of Directors. These Committees will be chaired by an Officer or Director or Committee Member as designated by the Board. The Chairman will proceed to select the remaining members of the Committee up to the number set by the Board or terminate the memberships or appoint successors at the Chairman's discretion. The Board may terminate any Committee by resolution.

Standing Functionary Committee

7.02 The Corporation will have the following Standing Functionary Committees, each of which will be chaired by a committee member, and may consist of persons who are not Directors of the Corporation appointed by the President:

(1) A Fund-raising Committee consisting of at least one Director

(2) A Media Committee

(3) A Filming and Photography Committee

(4) An Equipment and Tack Committee

ARTICLE VIII

OPERATIONS

Fiscal Year

8.01 The fiscal year of this corporation will be the calendar year.

Execution of Documents

8.02 Except as otherwise provided by law, checks, drafts, promissory notes, orders for the payment of money, and other evidences of indebtedness of this Corporation will be signed by the Treasurer and countersigned by the President. Contracts, leases, or other instruments executed in the name of and on behalf of the Corporation will be signed by the Secretary and countersigned by the President, and will have attached copies of the resolutions of the Board of Directors certified by the Secretary authorizing their execution.

Books and Records

8.03 This Corporation will keep correct and complete books and records of account, and will also keep minutes of the proceedings of its Board of Directors, Executive Committees and standing Functionary Committee. The Corporation will keep at its principal place of business a register giving the names and addresses of the Directors, Officers, and Committee Members, and the original or a copy of its Bylaws including

Inspection of Books and Records

8.04 All books and records of this Corporation may be inspected by any Director, or his agent or attorney, for any proper purpose at any reasonable time on written demand under oath, stating the purpose of the inspection.

Nonprofit Operations

8.05 This Corporation will not have or issue shares of stock. No dividend will be paid, and no part of the income of this Corporation will be distributed to its Directors or Officers. However, the Corporation may pay compensation in a reasonable amount to Officers, Directors, or Committee Members for services rendered.

Loans to Management

8.06 This Corporation will make no loans to any of its Directors, Officers, or Committee Members.

ARTICLE IX

AMENDMENT

Modification of Bylaws

9.01 The power to alter, amend, or repeal these Bylaws, or to adopt new Bylaws, to the extent allowed by law, is vested in the Board of Directors by a majority vote of same.

Adoption of Bylaws

9.02 Adopted by the Board of Directors by resolution and vote of _____.
                                                Date

_____

Signature

_____

Signature

_____

Signature

        Directors dissenting:

THE BEST GUIDE FOR NONPROFIT CORPORATIONS

SAMPLE RELIGIOUS BYLAWS

BYLAWS OF

_____

(insert your corporation name here)

A Nonprofit Corporation

ARTICLE I

OFFICES

The principal office of the corporation, hereinafter referred to as the "Church" shall be located at the address set forth in the Articles of Incorporation. The Church may have such other offices, either within or without the State of Incorporation, as the Board of Directors may determine from time to time.

ARTICLE II

STATEMENTS OF FAITH AND DOCTRINE

The Holy Bible is the inspired Word of God and is the basis for any statement of Faith. We believe the whole Bible to be the "Word of God," from *Genesis* to *Revelation*. Uplifting and upholding all the commandments given down by "God Himself" to Moses while being under the law.

Now being under "Grace and Truth" as stated in John 1:17. For the law was given by Moses, but Grace and Truth came by Jesus Christ. We band ourselves together as a body of baptized believers in Jesus Christ personally committed to sharing the good news of Salvation to lost mankind.

The Church accepts the Scriptures as the revealed Will of God, the all-sufficient rule of faith and practice, and, for the purpose of maintaining general unity, adopts these Statements of Fundamental Truths and Doctrine.

Section 1. The Scriptures Inspired.

The Bible is the inspired Word of God, a revelation from God to man, the infallible rule of faith and conduct, and is superior to conscience and reason, but not contrary to reason. (2 Tim. 3:15-17; 1 Peter 1:23-25; Heb. 4:12)

Section 2. The One True Godhead.

The triune Godhead is composed of three (3) separate and distinct personalities, The Father, The Son, and The Holy Spirit, who are eternally self-existent, self-revealed, and function as one entity. Jesus Christ, who is God manifested in the flesh, is the second member of the Godhead, co-equal and co-eternal with The Father and The Holy Spirit.

Section 3. Man, His Fall, and Redemption.

Man was created good and upright, for God said, "Let us make man in Our image, after Our likeness." But man, by voluntary transgression, fell, and his only hope of redemption is in Jesus Christ the Son of God. (Genesis 1:26-31, 3:1-7; Romans 5:12-21)

Section 4. The Salvation of Man.

(a) Man's only hope of redemption is through the shed blood of Jesus Christ. On the cross Jesus Christ became sin and sickness providing both salvation and divine healing for all mankind (Psalms 103:3), being justified freely by His Grace through the redemption that is in Christ Jesus. "For by grace we are saved through faith." "The word is near you, in your mouth and in your heart – that is, the word of faith which we are preaching, that if you confess with your mouth Jesus as Lord, and believe in your heart that God raised Him from the dead, you shall be saved; for with the heart man believes, resulting in righteousness, and with the mouth he confesses, resulting in salvation." (Romans 3:24; Ephesians 2:8; Romans 10:8-10)

b) The evidence of Salvation. The inward evidence to the believer of his salvation, is the direct witness of the Spirit. (Romans 8:16) The outward evidence to all men is a life of righteousness and true holiness. "And this is His commandment, that we believe in the name of His Son Jesus Christ, and love one another, just as He commanded us." (1 John 3:23)

(c) Faith and Works. Salvation is by faith in Jesus Christ and not by human works; however, our works will determine the rewards in eternity. (Romans 10:9-1 and 2 Cor. 5:10)

Section 5. Baptism in Water.

The ordinance of baptism by a burial with Christ should be observed as commanded in the Scriptures by all who have really repented and in their hearts have truly believed in Christ as Savior and Lord. In so doing, they declare to the world that they have died with Jesus and that they have also been raised with Him to walk in newness of life. (Matt. 28:19; Acts 10:47, 48; Romans 6:4)

Section 6. The Lord's Supper.

"And when He had given thanks, He broke it, and said, 'This is my body which is for you. Do this in remembrance of me.' In the same way also the cup, after supper, saying, 'This cup is the new covenant in my blood. Do this, as often as you drink it, in remembrance of me.' Let a man examine himself, and so eat of the bread and drink of the cup." (1 Cor. 11:24; 25, 28)

Section 7. The Promise of the Father.

All believers are entitled to, and should ardently expect and earnestly seek, the promise of the Father, the Baptism in the Holy Ghost and Fire, according to the command of our Lord Jesus Christ. This was the normal experience of all in the early Christian church. With it comes the endowment of power for life and service, the bestowment of the gifts and their uses in the work of the ministry. (Luke 24:49; Acts 1:4-8; 1 Cor. 12:1-31) This wonderful experience is distinct from and subsequent to the experience of the new birth. (Acts 2:38; 10:44-46; 11:14-16; 15:7-9)

Section 8. The Evidence of the Baptism in the Holy Spirit.

The full consummation of the Baptism of believers in the Holy Spirit is evidenced by the initial physical sign of speaking with other tongues as the Spirit gives utterance, and by the subsequent manifestation of spiritual power in public testimony and service. (Acts 2:4; 10:44-46; 19:2, 6; 1:8)

Section 9. The Church.

The church is the body of Christ, the habitation of God through the Spirit, with divine appointments for the fulfillment of her great commission. Each believer, born of the Spirit, is an integral part of the general assembly and church of the firstborn, which are written in Heaven. (Ephesians 1:22; 2:19-22; Hebrews 12:23)

Section 10. Total Prosperity.

(a) Spiritual. John 3:3, 11; 2 Cor. 5:17-21; Romans 10:9-10

(b) Mental. 2 Tim. 1:7; Romans 12:2; Isaiah 26:3

(c) Physical. Isaiah 53:4, 5; Matt. 8:17; 1 Peter 2:24

(d) Financial. 3 John 1:2; Malachi 3:10-11; Luke 6:38; 2 Cor. 9:6-10; Deut. 28:1-14

(e) Social. Proverbs 3:4

Section 11. Blessed Hope.

Jesus is coming again to gather all His Saints to Heaven. (1 Cor. 15:51-52; 1 Thess. 4:16-17; and 2 Thess. 2:1)

Section 12. The Millennial Reign of Jesus.

The return of our Lord Jesus Christ with His Saints from Heaven to rule and reign for 1,000 years on earth as the Scriptures promised. (Romans 11:25, 27; 2 Thess. 1:7; Rev. 19:11-16; 20:1-7) After this, there shall be a new heaven and a new earth. (Rev. 21)

ARTICLE III

NONPROFIT RELIGIOUS PURPOSES

_____, Inc., a Corporation, is a church, and in addition operates or may operate a school, a publishing division, a division that distributes charitable merchandise, and other divisions which further the religious purposes of the Corporation.

The property of the Corporation is irrevocably dedicated to nonprofit religious purposes. No part of the net earnings of the Corporation shall inure to the benefit of its directors, officers, private shareholders, or to any other individual, except that the Corporation shall be authorized and empowered to pay reasonable compensation for services rendered, and to make payment in the furtherance of the nonprofit religious purposes of the Corporation.

No substantial part of the activities of this Corporation shall consist of carrying on propaganda, or otherwise attempting to influence legislation, and this corporation shall not participate in or intervene in (including publishing or distributing statements) any political campaign on behalf of any candidate for public office.

Upon the winding up and dissolution of the Corporation, the Board of Directors shall, after adequately providing for all the debts, obligations, and liabilities of the Corporation, distribute the remaining assets of the Corporation exclusively for the nonprofit religious purposes of the Corporation and which are tax exempt under 501(C)(3) of the Internal Revenue Code, as the Board of Directors in its sole discretion shall determine.

In furtherance of its religious nonprofit tax-exempt purposes, the Corporation shall have the following powers and authority.

(a) To do all acts, perform all functions, and carry on all activities permitted by the nonprofit corporation laws of the State of Florida, or of any other state in which the Corporation is qualified to act.

(b) To have and exercise all powers and rights enjoyed by corporations generally in the Sate of Florida, and in any state in which the Corporation is qualified to act, as long as the exercise of such powers is not specifically prohibited for nonprofit religious corporations.

(c) To use all media, whether now known or hereafter discovered, including, but not limited to, print, television, and radio.

(d) To exercise such incidental powers as may reasonably be necessary to carry out the purposes for which the Corporation is established, provided that such incidental powers shall be exercised in a manner consistent with its tax-exempt status as a religious organization as set forth in Section 501(C)(3) of the Code.

(e) Notwithstanding any other provisions of the Articles of Incorporation or these Bylaws, the Corporation shall not, except to an insubstantial degree, engage in any activity or exercise any powers that are not in furtherance of the nonprofit religious purposes of the Corporation, and the corporation shall not carry on any activity not permitted to be carried on (a) by a corporation exempt from Federal income tax under Section 501(C)(3) of the Code, or under the corresponding section of any future United States revenue law; or (b) by a corporation, contributions to which are deductible under 170(b)(1)(A)(i) and 170(c)(2) of the Code, or the corresponding section of any future United States revenue law.

Membership

Section 1. Candidacy

Any person may offer himself/herself as a candidate for membership in this church, after sufficient counseling by the Pastor, staff, and/or in any of the following ways:

a) By profession of faith in our Lord Jesus Christ, and for baptism according to the policies of this church.

(b) By promise of a letter.

(c) By restoration upon a statement of prior conversion experience and baptism when no letter is obtainable.

(d) If candidate has been scripturally immersed by another denomination and feels that his/her baptism was scriptural in every way, and believes that the Bible teaches only one baptism, thus making it unscriptural to be baptized again, and states same to the Pastor. The Pastor may recommend to the church that candidate be accepted as a member without being baptized again; the church may then agree to forego baptism.

Any applicant shall give clear evidence of their new birth in Christ, live a consistent Christian life, and worship at the Church on a regular basis for at least a three- (3) month continuous period, support the Church financially, and subscribe to the Tenets of Faith as defined by these Bylaws.

Section 2: Voting Rights of Members

The Corporation hereby elects to have no voting members.

All rights which otherwise would vest in the members shall vest in Board of Directors.

Section 3: Discipline

(A) It shall be the basic purpose of the _____, Inc. to emphasize to its members that every reasonable measure will be taken to assist any troubled member. The Pastor, other members of the church staff, and Deacons are available for counsel and guidance. Redemption rather than punishment should be the guideline which governs the attitude of one member toward another.

(B) Should some serious condition exist which would cause a member to become a liability to the general welfare of the church , every reasonable measure will be taken by the Pastor and the Deacons to resolve the problem. All such proceedings shall be pervaded by a spirit of Christian kindness and forbearance. But, finding that the welfare of the church will best be served by the exclusion of the member, the church may take this action by a two-thirds vote of the members present at a meeting called for this purpose; and the church may proceed to declare the offender to be no longer in the membership of the church.

ARTICLE IV

CHURCH OFFICERS – CALLED

All church officers must be members of the church. The officers shall be as follows:

President _____

Vice President _____

Secretary _____

Treasurer _____

Trustee _____

Section 1: The President, 1st Vice President, 2nd Vice President, and Secretary may sign checks or drafts of the organization.

Pastor/President

The pastor is responsible for leading the church. The pastor will lead the congregation, the organizations, and the church officers to perform their tasks.

The pastor is the leader of all pastoral ministries in this church. As such, he works with the Deacons and the church staff to:

(A)   Lead the church in performing its tasks

(B)   Lead the church to engage in a fellowship of worship, witness, education, ministry, and application

(C)   Proclaim the Gospel to believers and unbelievers

(D)   Care for the church's members and other persons in the community

Vice President

A Vice President's responsibility shall be to assist the pastor in all of his duties and to assume the full responsibility of the pastor in his absence with all powers as if he/she had been duly elected President.

Treasurer

The nominating committee shall nominate no fewer than two lay people for this position. The treasurer shall keep accounts of all money of the corporation received or disbursed, and shall render to the church at each regular business meeting a monthly financial report for the preceding month. The treasurer will serve on the finance committee, but can never be chairperson. It is the responsibility of the treasurer to ensure the integrity of all accounts, and only disburse those funds as determined by the church. The Treasurer shall have the care and custody of all monies belonging to the organization and shall be solely responsible for such monies or securities of the organization. He/She shall cause to be deposited in a regular business bank or trust company a sum not exceeding $_____, and the balance of the funds of the organization shall be deposited in a savings bank except that the Board of

Directors may cause such funds to be invested in such investments as shall be legal for a savings bank in the State of Florida. He/She may be one of the officers who shall sign checks or drafts of the organization. No special fund may be set aside that shall make it unnecessary for the Treasurer to sign the checks issued upon it. He/She shall render at stated periods as the Board of Directors shall determine a written account of the finances of the organization, and such report shall be physically affixed to the minutes of Board of Directors of such meeting.

Business Administration

The business administrator is responsible for the smooth and efficient daily operation of the church's physical assets; shall coordinate with the personnel committee the needs of the church staff and other paid staff; e.g. custodians, maintenance workers, secretaries, and bookkeepers. The business administrator will provide the daily supervision of the church's financial assets as directed by the Financial committee. He/She will coordinate with the pastoral staff, church committees, and personnel committees, and submit a recommended annual budget to the Finance committee no later than 90 days prior to the start of the church's fiscal year.

Secretary

The Secretary shall keep the minutes and records of the organization in appropriate books, and file any certificate required by any statute, federal or state. He/She shall give and serve all notices to members of this organization. He/She shall be the official custodian of the records and seal of this corporation. He/She may be one of the officers required to sign the checks and drafts of the organization. He/She shall present to the membership at any meetings any communication addressed to him/her as Secretary of the organization.

ARTICLE V

CHURCH STAFF AND OTHER PAID PERSONNEL

This church shall call or employ such staff members as the church shall need. A job description shall be written by the business administrator when the need for staff members is determined. Vocational staff members other than the Pastor shall be recommended to the church by the personnel committee.

ARTICLE VI

ELECTED CHURCH OFFICERS

Deacons

There may be four deacons for the first 100 members and one deacon for each 25 members thereafter. These men shall meet the qualifications set forth in 1 Timothy, Chapter 3, and shall be ordained according to the teaching of the New Testament.

Three or more deacons elected by the church will hold in trust the church property. They shall have no power to buy, sell, mortgage, lease, or transfer any property without a specific vote of the Board of Directors to affix their signatures to legal documents involving the sale, mortgage, purchase, or rental of the property or other legal documents where the signatures of deacons are required. All legal documents shall be kept in the church office in a safe place.

The deacons shall serve at the pleasure of the President, but have no voting privileges. A list of all men/women both scripturally qualified and willing to serve shall be published by the Deacons two weeks prior to the elections. The list shall contain at a minimum more names than the number to be elected. The Deacons will consult with and assist the Pastor in spiritual activities and assist with the administration of the ordinances. They will make recommendations to the church concerning all matters decided upon by them except in cases where the church has given them authority to take final action. The Deacons shall equitably apportion the church members for the purpose of becoming and remaining familiar with them and their spiritual and economical problems; act as counselor and guide to them under the direction of the Pastor; tend to the needy of the needs of the membership as the budget provides and/or permits.

Church Clerk

The nominating committee shall nominate no less than two lay people for this position. A paid church employee is not eligible for this position. The church-elected clerk of the church shall keep a suitable book as a record of all the actions of the church and minutes of all business meetings, except as otherwise herein provided. This person is responsible for keeping a register of the names of the members, with dates of admission, dismissal, or death, together with a record of baptisms. This person shall issue letters of dismissal voted by the church, preserve on file all communications and written official reports, and give legal notice of all meetings where such notice is necessary, as indicated in these bylaws. The church may delegate some of the clerical responsibilities to a church secretary. All church records are church property and shall be filed in the church office in a safe place.

Sunday School Superintendent

The nominating committee shall nominate two candidates for Sunday School. It is the responsibility of the Sunday School Director to select candidates for the nominating committee to serve as Sunday School teachers.

Missionary/Evangelistic Department

The President of the Missionary/Evangelistic Department shall lead and direct the missionary to carry out their responsibilities as specified in this constitution.

Minister of Music

The minister of music will be responsible for the enlistment and proper functioning of the church's music program; e.g., adult choir, instrumental program, special music, and special musical programs.

Minister of Youth

The minister of youth stimulates, coordinates, evaluates, and aids the youth of the church through the membership of the various program organizations of the church, and directly through special projects and/or programs approved by the church. Additionally, the minister of youth will coordinate the activities of the youth council and will develop a youth calendar of activities, events, retreats, seminars, and so forth.

ARTICLE VII

BOARD OF DIRECTORS INDEMNIFICATION

Section 1. Indemnification.

The Corporation shall, to the maximum extent permitted by Florida Corporation law, indemnify each of its agents against expenses, judgments, fines, settlements, and other amounts actually and reasonably incurred in connection with any proceeding arising by reason of the fact any such person is or was an agent of the Corporation. For purposes of this Article, an "agent" of the Corporation includes any person who is or was a Director, Officer, employee, or other agent of the Corporation, or is or was serving at the request of the Corporation as a Director, Officer, employee, or agent of a corporation which was a predecessor corporation of the Corporation or of another enterprise at the request of such predecessor corporation.

Section 2. Non-Assessability.

The private property of the Directors and Officers of the Corporation shall be non-assessable and shall not be subject to the payment of any corporate debts, nor shall the Directors or Officers of the Corporation become individually liable or responsible for any debts or liabilities of the Corporation.

CONFERENCE TELEPHONE

Members of the Board may participate in a meeting through the use of a conference telephone or similar communications equipment, as long as all members participating in such meeting can hear one another. Participation in a meeting via conference call constitutes presence in person at such meeting.

Section 1. General Powers.

The affairs of the Church shall be managed by the Board of Directors, whose members shall have a fiduciary obligation to the Church.

Section 2. Number, Term, and Qualifications.

The number of Directors shall be no less than three (3) and shall have no maximum number. The term of membership shall be for two (2) years, except for the Pastor-President. Those set forth in the Articles of Incorporation shall comprise the original Board of Directors. Any member of the Board of Directors must also be a member of the congregation of the Church.

Section 3. Regular Meetings.

A regular meeting of the Board of Directors shall be held each year. The Board of Directors may provide, by resolution, the time and place for holding additional regular meetings without other notice than such resolution. Additional regular meetings shall be held at the principal office of the Church in the absence of any designation in the resolution.

Section 4. Special Meetings.

Special Meetings of the Board of Directors may be called by or at the request of any two (2) Directors, and shall be held at the principal office of the Church or at such other place as the Directors may determine.

Section 5. Notice of the annual, regular, or any special meeting of the Board of Directors shall be given by oral notice to each Director.

The attendance of a Director at any meeting shall constitute a waiver of notice of such meeting, except where a Director attends a meeting for the express purpose of objecting to the transaction of any business because the meeting is not lawfully called or convened. The business to be transacted at the meeting need not be specified in the notice or waiver of notice of such meeting, unless specifically required by law or by these Bylaws.

Section 6. Action by Unanimous Written Consent Without Meeting.

Any action required or permitted to be taken by the Board of Directors under any provision of law may be taken without a meeting, if all members of the Board shall individually or collectively consent in writing to such action. Such written consent or consents shall be filed with the minutes of the proceedings of the Board. Such action by written consent shall have the same force and effect as the unanimous vote of the Directors. Any certificate or other document filed under any provision of law which relates to action so taken shall state that the action was taken by unanimous written consent of the Board of Directors without a meeting and that the Bylaws of this corporation authorize the directors to so act, and such statement shall be *prima facie* evidence of such authority.

Section 7. Quorum.

A majority of the Board of Directors shall constitute a quorum for the transaction of business at any meeting of the Board; but if less than a majority of the Directors are present at any meeting, a majority of the Directors present may adjourn the meeting from time to time without further notice.

Section 8. Board Decisions.

The act of a majority of the Directors present at a meeting at which a quorum is present shall be the act of the Board of Directors, unless the act of a greater number is required by law or by these Bylaws.

Section 9. Vacancies, Additions, Elections, and Removal.

Any vacancy occurring on the Board of Directors and any directorship to be filled by reason of an increase in the number of Directors, shall be filled by the Pastor with the advice and consent of a majority of the present Board of Directors. Directors shall be removed by the Pastor/President with the advice and consent of the Board of Advisors. In the event all Director positions shall become vacant, the Board of Elders shall act as Interim Board of Directors until the vacancies are filled.

Section 10. Compensation.

Directors as such shall not receive any salaries for their services.

ARTICLE VIII

CHURCH POLICY

Section 1. Ecclesiastical Tribunal

The highest ecclesiastical tribunal within the Church shall be the Board of Directors of the Corporation. The Board of Directors shall be the express and final arbiter of ecclesiastical polity, doctrine, church discipline, and questions of church property. The Board of Directors shall elect to, in the near future, allow for a pension and insurance plan for the President/Pastor. The Board of Directors cannot vote to remove the President, except by resignation, by death, or by incapacitation.

ARTICLE IX

BOARD OF ADVISORS

Section 1. Board of Advisors.

A Board of Advisors may be appointed by the President, and shall serve at the pleasure of the President. Advisors shall give advice and counsel as requested by the President or the Board of Directors, but such advice and counsel shall not be binding either on the President or on the Board of Directors. Advisors shall not have any vote on the Board of Directors.

ARTICLE X

OFFICERS

Section 1. Employment Contract; Pastor/President.

It is the express desire of the Church to employ the Pastor/President pursuant to an Employment Contract that specifically addresses the duties and responsibilities of the Pastor/President, and the terms and conditions of such employment. In the event that the Church and Pastor/President are able to execute an Employment Contract, to the extent that any term, provision, or condition of any such contract conflicts with any part of these Bylaws, the language of the contract shall prevail. The Board of Directors, Board of Advisors, and Board of Elders are charged with the responsibility of negotiating an Employment Contract with the Pastor/President which is comprehensive and in the best interest of the Church.

Section 2. Officers.

The officers of the corporation shall be a Pastor/President, a secretary, a treasurer, one or more vice presidents, and such other officers as may be elected in accordance with the provisions of this Article. The Board of Directors may elect or appoint such other officers, including one or more assistant secretaries and one or more assistant treasurers, as it shall deem desirable, such officers to have the authority and perform the duties prescribed, from time to time, by the Board of Directors. Any two or more offices may be held by the same person.

Section 3. Election and Term of Office.

The officers of the Church shall be elected annually by the Board of Directors at the regular meeting of the Board of Directors. If the election of officers is not held at such meeting, such election shall be held as soon thereafter as is convenient. New offices may be created and filled at any meeting of the Board of Directors. Each officer shall hold office until his successor has been duly elected and qualified.

Section 4. Removal.

Any officer, with the exception of the Pastor/President, elected or appointed by the Board of Directors may be removed by the Board of Directors whenever in its judgment the best interests of the Church would be served thereby, but such removal shall be without prejudice to the contract rights, if any, of the officer so removed.

Section 5. Vacancies.

A vacancy in any office, except that of Pastor/President, because of death, resignation, removal, disqualification, or otherwise, may be filled by the Pastor for the unexpired portion of the term. In the event the vacant position being filled is that of the Pastor, the Board shall fill said position pursuant to Section 5 of this Article.

Section 6. Resignation, Removal of Pastor/President.

(a) Resignation. In the event the Pastor should voluntarily choose to leave, he shall designate his successor.

(b) Removal Without Cause. In the event that the Pastor has an Employment Contract with the Church, the Pastor may be removed without cause in accordance with the Removal Without Cause provisions of such contract.

(c) Removal for Cause. The Pastor may be removed for cause pursuant to the terms of any Employment Contract existing between the Pastor and the Church. In the absence of any such contract, the provisions of these Bylaws shall govern the removal of the Pastor. In the event the Pastor shall have serious charges preferred against him or his ministry has ceased to be effective, the matter shall be brought to the Board of Elders if such board exists and is active. If the Board of Elders does not exist or is inactive, such matter shall be taken to the Board of Directors. In the event the matter cannot be resolved at this meeting, power is then vested in the Board of Directors, the Board of Advisors, and the Board of Elders, to the extent that such boards exist and are active, to come together with the Pastor to consider his removal. Upon recommendation of removal by a unanimous vote of the combined voting members of such boards (not counting the vote of the Pastor as a member of any of the boards), this matter shall be referred to the members of the congregation for a vote. A greater than three-fourths (3/4) majority vote of the voting members of the congregation present at the meeting shall be required for removal. The Associate Pastor or some other person designated by agreement of the boards shall represent the combined boards and chair the meeting of the voting members of the congregation.

(d) Resignation. In the event the Pastor should voluntarily choose to leave, he shall designate his successor. Said designated successor shall be chosen with the advice and consent of the Board of Directors, the Board of Advisors, and the Board of Elders.

(e) Removal. In the event the Pastor shall have serious charges preferred against him or his ministry has ceased to be effective,

Section 7. Pastoral Recruitment and Confirmation.

In the event the Pastor shall resign or be removed, a special committee shall be appointed by the combined Board of Directors, Board of Advisors, and Board of Elders to recruit and present a candidate to the membership of the congregation for Pastor/President. This process shall be spiritually directed and accomplished as expeditiously as possible.

(a) Presentation. Upon recommendation of the special committee, the Pastor/President candidate shall be presented to the combined Board of Directors, Board of Advisors, and Board of Elders for their approval and recommendation. In the event two-thirds (2/3) of the combined Board of Directors, Board of Advisors, and Board of Elders shall approve said candidate, this matter shall be referred to the membership of the congregation for a vote.

(b) Final Approval. In the event a candidate for Pastor/President is approved by the combined Board of Directors, Board of Advisors, and Board of Elders, the membership of the congregation shall be called together to vote, by secret ballot, on said candidate. A two-thirds (2/3) majority vote of the members of the congregation shall be required to elect said candidate to office.

(c) Notice. A special notice procedure for all meetings referenced in this ARTICLE FIVE,

Section 5 shall apply as follows:

(i) Seven (7) days' notice in writing shall be provided for a combined Board of Directors, Board of Advisors, and Board of Elders meeting. Notice shall be given to each member of each Board and to the present Pastor/President.

(ii) Notice to the membership of the congregation of any congregational meetings shall be given orally at each Sunday service at least fourteen (14) days prior to such meeting and in writing by placing the announcement of said meeting in each Sunday bulletin during the same time frame.

Section 9. Quorum.

A majority of the total members of the Board of Directors, Board of Advisors, and Board of Elders shall constitute a quorum for their combined meetings as set forth in ARTICLE SEVEN, Section 7.

Section 10. Order of Business.

The order of business at the meeting of the members of the congregation shall be as follows:

a. Meeting called to order

b. Declaration of Quorum of Members present

c. Reading of the minutes of previous meeting for correction and /or adoption by membership

d. Treasurer's Report

e. Church Clerk's Report

f. Committee Reports

g. Program Organizations Report

h. Old and/or unfinished business

i. New Business

j. Adjournment

ARTICLE XI

POWERS OF OFFICERS

Section 1. The Pastor/President

The Church finds its headship under the Lord Jesus Christ, in its Pastor. The Pastor/President shall be the chief executive officer of the Church. He shall be a continuing member of the Board of Directors. He shall have general management of the business of the Church and general supervision of the other officers. He shall preside at all meetings of the Board of Directors and see that all orders and resolutions of the Board are carried into effect, subject, however, to the right of the Board to delegate to any other officer or officers of the Church any specific powers, other than those that may be conferred only upon the Pastor/President. He shall execute in the name of the Church all deeds, bonds, mortgages, contracts, and other documents authorized by the Board of Directors. He shall be an *ex-officio* member of all standing committees, and shall have the general powers and duties of supervision and management usually vested in the office of president of a corporation.

No person shall be invited to speak, teach, or minister in the Church without his approval. He shall be designated attorney-in-fact for the Church by virtue of his office. He shall have the authority to appoint and approve any assistants that would be necessary to properly carry out the work of the Lord.

(a) The Associate Pastor-Vice President: An Associate Pastor-Vice President shall perform the duties and exercise the powers of the Pastor/President in case of his temporary absence from the office of the Church, and shall perform such other duties as may from time to time be granted or imposed by the Board of Directors. He shall serve as an *ex-officio* member of the Board of Advisors; however, in the event of serving as interim Pastor/President, he shall be a voting member of the Board of Advisors.

(b) The Secretary: The Secretary shall attend all sessions of the Board held at the office of the Church and act as clerk thereof and record all votes and the minutes of all proceedings in a book to be kept for that purpose. He shall perform like duties for the executive and standing committees when required. He shall give, or cause to be given, notice of meetings of the Board of Directors when notice is required to be given under these Bylaws or by any resolution of the Board. He shall have custody of the seal and authority to execute all authorized documents requiring a seal. He shall keep the membership rolls of the Church, and in general perform the duties usually incident to the office of Secretary, and such further duties as shall from time to time be prescribed by the Board of Directors or the Pastor/President.

(c) The Treasurer: The Treasurer shall keep full and accurate account of the receipts and disbursements in books belonging to the Church, and shall deposit all monies and other valuable effects in the name and to the credit of the Church in such banks and depositories as may be designated by the Board of Directors, but shall not be personally liable for the safekeeping of any funds or securities so deposited pursuant to the order of the Board. He shall disburse the funds of the Church as may be ordered by the Board and shall render to the Pastor/President and Directors at the regular meeting of the Board, and whenever they may require, accounts of all his transactions as Treasurer and of the financial condition of the Church. He shall perform the duties usually incident to the office of Treasurer and such other duties as may be prescribed by the Board of Directors or by the Pastor/President.

(d) Delegating Powers to Other Officers: In case of the absence of any officer of the Church, or for any other reason that may seem sufficient to the Board, the Board of Directors may delegate his duties and powers from the time being to any other officer, or to any Director.

COMMITTEES, ELDERS, DEACONS, AND BOARD OF ADVISORS

Section 1. Committees of Directors.

The Board of Directors, by resolution adopted by a majority of the Directors in office, may designate one or more committees which, to the extent provided in such resolution, shall have and exercise the authority of the Board of Directors in the management of the Church; but the designation of such committees and the delegation thereto of authority shall not operate to relieve the Board of Directors, or any individual Director, of any responsibility imposed on it or him by law.

Section 2. Other Committees.

Other committees not having and exercising the authority of the Board of Directors in the management of the Church may be designated by a resolution adopted by a majority of the Directors present at a meeting at which a quorum is present. Except as otherwise provided in such resolution, members of each such committee shall be members of the congregation of the Church, and the Pastor shall appoint the members thereof. Any member thereof may be removed by the person or persons authorized to appoint such member whenever, in their judgment, the best interests of the Church shall be served by such removal.

Section 3. Elders and Deacons.

Elders and/or Deacons may be chosen by the Board of Directors from the membership of the congregation of the Church who demonstrate that their lives conform to the Scriptural qualifications thereof .(1 Tim. 3:2-7; Titus 1:6-9; 1 Peter 5:2-3) The Board of Elders shall rule and teach. The Board of Elders shall consist of those Heads of Departments in the Church which are designated by the Pastor. Elders and Deacons shall function to provide spiritual support to the Pastor in the discipleship of new converts, praying for the sick (James 5:14), encouraging and developing spiritual gifts and ministries in the body, and to assist in the administration of the ordinances of the Church. Their number and term of office shall not be predetermined. They shall have no vote on the Board of Directors; however, shall give counsel and mutual assistance to the Board of Directors and the Pastor in the administration of business and work of the Church as specifically assigned by the Pastor.

Section 4. Board of Advisors.

A Board of Advisors may be appointed as set forth below. It shall be the responsibility and privilege of the Board of Advisors to provide Godly counsel to the Pastor/President and the Board of Directors. Counsel shall be in organizational, financial, legal, or other areas wherein the Pastor/President determines professional counsel is needed and/or desirable. No minimum or maximum number of members of the Board of Advisors shall be established, and the appointment to the Board and tenure hereon shall be at the pleasure and in the complete discretion of the Pastor/President. The advice and consent of the Board of Advisors shall be required to establish and/or change salary and other compensation payable to the Pastor by the Board of Directors.

MINISTERS

Section 1. Ordination and Licensing.

The Board of Directors may ordain and/or license a person as minister of the Gospel after first examining the applicant's background, moral and religious character, and the previous Bible course and/or independent study applicant has received. Final determination shall be at the absolute discretion of the Board of Directors.

Section 2. Limitation.

The Board of Directors may, at the discretion of the Board, limit any licensee or ordainee to an area of special emphasis. The following areas (although not intended to be inclusive) are recognized by the Board of Directors:

(a) *Minister of Music* - The Minister of Music will be responsible for the enlistment and proper functioning of the church's music program; e.g., adult choir, instrumental program, special music, and special musical programs.

(b) *Minister of Youth* - The Minister of Youth shall stimulate, coordinate, evaluate, and aid the youth of the church through the leadership of the various program organizations of the church, and directly through special projects and/or programs approved by church action. Additionally, the Minister of Youth will coordinate the activities of the youth council and will develop a youth calendar of activities, events, retreats, seminars, and so forth.

(c) *Christian Education and Church Training* - There shall be a church training program divided into departments for all ages and conducted under the direction of a Minister. The tasks of the training shall be to orientate new church members, train church members to perform the functions of the church, train church leaders, teach Christian theology, Christian ethics, Christian history, and church policies and organizations' provide and interpret information regarding the work of the church and denomination.

(d) *Outreach Ministry-* There shall be a outreach ministry under the direction of the Minister of Outreach, who shall direct, instruct, coordinate various outreach ministries that function in/outside of the church.

Section 3. Pastor/President.

The Pastor/President shall be a licensed or ordained minister of the Gospel. Assistant or associate ministers may or may not be either licensed or ordained (example – assistant may be a spouse of an ordained Pastor.)

Section 4. Application.

Application for ordination and/or licensing as a minister of the Gospel shall be on the form provided by the Board of Directors. An applicant's application shall be either approved or denied within thirty (30) days of the completion of the investigation of the applicant. Those applicants who are approved shall receive a certificate evidencing the approval.

Section 5. School of Ministry.

The Board of Directors may establish a School of Ministry, setting forth a prescribed curriculum and course of study leading to ordination and licensing of ministers. The School of Ministry shall prepare the student in the knowledge of the Word of God and in ministering to the needs of mankind through the Gospel of Jesus Christ.

Section 1. Indemnification, Insurance, and Liability Indemnification of Church Pastor, Officers, Directors, and Other Persons

The Church shall advance necessary funds or indemnify any person who was or is a party or is threatened to be made a party to any threatened, pending, or completed action, suit, or proceeding, whether civil, criminal, administrative, or investigative (other than an action by or in the right of the Church) by reason of the fact that the person is or was the Church's pastor, a director or officer of the Church, or is or was serving at the request of the Church as a director or officer of another corporation, partnership, joint venture, trust, or other enterprise, against expenses (including attorneys' fees), judgments, fines, and amounts paid in settlement actually and reasonably incurred by the person in connection with such threatened, pending, or completed action, suit, or proceeding. The termination of any action, suit, or proceeding by judgment, order, settlement, or conviction or upon a plea of *nolo contendere* or its equivalent, shall not, of itself, create a presumption that the person did not act in good faith and in a manner which he reasonably believed to be in or not opposed to the best interests of the Church, and, with respect to any criminal action or proceeding, had reasonable cause to believe that his conduct was unlawful.

Section 2.

The Church shall advance funds or indemnify any person who is a party or is threatened to be made a party to any threatened, pending, or completed action or suit by or in the right of the Church to procure a judgment in its favor by reason of the fact that he is or was a pastor, director, or officer of the Church, or is or was serving at the request of the Church as a director, officer, or representative of another corporation, partnership, joint venture, trust, or other enterprise against expenses (including attorneys' fees), judgments, fines, and amounts paid in settlement, actually and reasonably incurred by the person in connection with such threatened, pending, or completed action or suit by or in the right of the Church.

Section 3.

Indemnification under Sections 1 and 2 of this Article shall be automatic and shall not require any determination that indemnification is proper, except that no indemnification shall be made in any case where the act or failure to act giving rise to the claim for indemnification is determined by a court of competent jurisdiction to have constituted willful misconduct or recklessness.

Section 4.

Expenses incurred in defending a civil or criminal action, suit, or proceeding of the kind described in Sections 1 and 2 of this Article shall be paid by the Church in advance of the final disposition of such action, suit, or proceeding upon receipt of an undertaking, by or on behalf of the person who may be entitled to indemnification under those Sections, to repay such amount unless it shall ultimately be determined that he is entitled to be indemnified by the Church.

Section 5.

The Church may, at the discretion of and to the extent and for such persons as determined by the Board of Directors of the Church, (1) indemnify any person who neither is nor was the Church's pastor, a director, or officer of the Church but who is or was a party or is threatened to be made a party to any threatened, pending, or completed action, suit, or proceeding, whether civil, criminal, administrative, or investigative (and whether brought by or in the right of the Church), by reason of the fact that the person is or was a representative of the Church, against expenses (including attorneys' fees), judgments, fines, and amounts paid in settlement, actually and reasonably incurred by the person in connection with such threatened, pending or completed action, suit, or proceeding; and (2) pay such expenses in advance of the final disposition of such action, suit, or proceeding, upon receipt of an undertaking by or on behalf of such person to repay such amount if it shall ultimately be determined by a court of competent jurisdiction that such person is not entitled to be indemnified by the Church.

Section 6.

Any right to indemnification provided in this Article shall continue to a person who has ceased to be a pastor, director, or officer of the Church and shall inure to the benefit of the heirs, executors, and administrators of such a person.

Section 7.

Nothing herein contained shall be construed as limiting the power or obligation of the Church to indemnify any person in accordance with applicable state law provisions as amended from time to time or in accordance with any similar law adopted in lieu thereof.

Section 8.

The Church shall also indemnify any person against expenses (including attorneys' fees), actually and reasonably incurred by him in enforcing any right to indemnification under this Article, under the Church's state nonprofit corporation law as amended from time to time or under any similar law adopted in lieu thereof.

Section 9.

Any person who shall serve as the Church's Pastor/President, a director, officer, employee, or agent of the Church or who shall serve at the request of the Church, as a director, officer, employee, or agent of another corporation, joint partnership, joint venture trust, or other enterprise shall be deemed to do so with knowledge of and in reliance upon the rights of indemnification provided in this Article, under applicable state law indemnification provisions as amended from time to time and in or under any similar law adopted in lieu thereof.

The Church shall have the power to purchase and maintain insurance on behalf of any person who is or was the Church's Pastor/President, a director, officer, employee, or agent of the Church or is or was serving at the request of the Church as a director, officer, employee, or agent of another corporation, partnership, joint venture, trust, or other enterprise against any liability asserted against him and incurred by him in any such capacity, or arising out of his status as such, whether or not the Church would have the power to indemnify him against such liability.

LIABILITY OF OFFICERS AND BOARD MEMBERS

To the fullest extent permitted by applicable state law, as now in effect and as amended from time to time, the Church's Pastor/President, or a director or officer of the Church shall not be personally liable for monetary damages for any action taken or failure to take any action.

DIRECTORS' LIABILITY

Section 1.

A director of the Church shall stand in a fiduciary relationship to the Church and shall perform his duties as a director, including his duties as a member of any committee of the Board upon which he may serve, in good faith, in a manner he reasonably believes to be in the best interests of the Church, and with such care, including reasonable inquiry, skill, and diligence, as a person of ordinary prudence would use under similar circumstances. In performing his duties, a director or committee member shall be entitled to rely in good faith on information, opinions, reports, or statements, including financial statements and other financial data, in each case prepared by any of the following:

(a) One or more officers or employees of the Church whom the director reasonably believes to be reliable and competent in the matters presented;

(b) Counsel, public accountants, or other persons as to matters which the director reasonably believes to be reliable and competent in the matters presented;

(c) A committee of the Board of Directors upon which he does not serve, duly designated in accordance with law, as to matters within its designated authority, which the director reasonably believes to merit confidence.

Section 2.

The Church's Pastor/President or director shall not be considered to be acting in good faith if he has knowledge concerning the matter in question that would cause his reliance to be unwarranted.

Section 3.

In discharging the duties of their respective positions, the Pastor/President, the Board of Directors, committees of the Board of Directors, and the individual directors thereof may, in considering the best interests of the Church, consider the effects of any action upon employees, suppliers, and customers of the Church and upon communities in which offices or other establishments of the Church are located, and all other pertinent factors. The consideration of those factors shall not constitute a violation of this section.

Section 4.

Absent breach of fiduciary duty, lack of good faith or self-dealing, actions taken as the Church's Pastor/President, director, or officer, or any failure to take any action shall presumed to be in the best interests of the Church. The Church's Pastor/President, director, or officer of the Church shall not be personally liable for monetary damages as such for any action taken, or any failure to take any action, unless:

(a) The Pastor/President, officer, or director has breached or failed to perform the duties of his office under this section or under the specific provisions of any employment agreement with the Church;

(b) The breach or failure to perform constitutes self-dealing, willful misconduct, or recklessness.

Section 5.

The provisions of this section shall not apply to:

(a) The responsibility or liability of the Church's Pastor/President, officer, or director pursuant to any criminal statute; or

(b) The liability of the Church's Pastor/President, officer, or director for the payment of taxes pursuant to local, state, or federal law.

CONTRACT OF FINANCIAL INTEREST DIRECTORS

Section 1.

No contract or transaction between the Church and its Pastor/President or one or more of its directors or officers, or between the Church and any other corporation in which its Pastor/President or one or more of its directors or officers are also directors or officers or have a financial interest shall be void or voidable solely for such reason, or solely because the Pastor/President or director or officer is present or participates in the meeting of the Board which authorizes the contract or transaction, or solely because his or their votes are counted for such purpose, if:

(a) The material facts as to his interest and as to the contract or transaction are disclosed or known to the Board of Directors and the Chairman of the Board in good faith authorizes the contract or transaction; or

(b) The contract or transaction is fair as to the Church as of the time it is authorized, approved, or ratified by the Chairman of the Board of Directors.

Section 2.

Interested directors may be counted in determining the presence of a quorum at a meeting of the Board of Directors which authorizes a contract or transaction in the preceding section.

CONTRACTS, CHECKS, DEPOSITS AND FUNDS

Section 1. Contracts.

The Board of Directors may authorize any officer or officers, agent or agents of the Church, in addition to the officers so authorized by these Bylaws, to enter into any contract or execute and deliver any instrument in the name of and on behalf of the Church, and such authority may be general or may be confined to specific instances.

Section 2. Checks, Drafts, or Orders.

All checks, drafts, or orders for the payment of money, notes, or other evidences of indebtedness issued in the name of the Church shall be signed by such officer or officers, agent or agents of the Church, and in such manner as shall from time to time be determined by resolution of the Board of Directors. In the absence of such determination by the Board of Directors, such instruments may be signed by either the Treasurer or the Pastor of the Church.

Section 3. Deposits.

All funds of the Church shall be deposited from time to time to the credit of the Church in such banks, trust companies, or other depositories as the Board of Directors may select.

Section 4. Gifts.

The Board of Directors may accept on behalf of the Church any contribution, gift, bequest, or device for any purpose of the Church. (Mal. 3:10; Luke 6:38; 1 Cor. 16:1; and 2 Cor. 9:6-8)

BOOKS AND RECORDS

The Church shall keep correct and complete books and records of account and shall also keep minutes of the proceedings of its members, Board of Directors, committees having and exercising any of the authority of the Board of Directors, and any other committee, and shall keep at the principal office a record giving the names and addresses of the Board of Directors members entitled to vote. All books and records of the Church may be inspected by any member, or his agent, for any proper purpose at any reasonable time.

FISCAL YEAR

The fiscal year of the Church shall be the calendar year: Begin the first of January and close the 31st of December.

The church year (for anniversary purposes) shall begin the first of _____ and close the 31st of _____.

DISSOLUTION

Section 1.

Upon the dissolution of the Church, the Board of Directors shall, after the payment of all the liabilities of the Church, dispose of all of the assets of the Church exclusively for the purposes of the Church in such manner, or to such organization or organizations organized and operated exclusively for the purposes of the Church in such manner, or to such organization or organizations organized and operated exclusively for charitable, educational, religious, or scientific purposes as shall qualify as an exempt corporation or organizations under Section 501(C)(3) of the Internal Revenue Code of 1986, as amended (or of the corresponding provisions of any future United States Revenue Law) as the Board of Directors shall determine.

Section 2.

No part of the net earnings of the Church shall inure to the benefit of, or be distributable to, its members, officers, directors, or any person except that the Church shall be authorized and empowered to pay reasonable compensation for services rendered, and to make payments in the furtherance of the Church. Notwithstanding any other provisions of the Articles of Incorporation or these Bylaws of the Church, the Church shall not carry on any activity not permitted to be carried on (1) by a corporation exempt from Federal Income Tax, under Section 501(C)(3) of the Internal Revenue Code of 1986, as amended (or by the corresponding section of any future Revenue Code of the United States of America); or (2) by a corporation, contributions of which are deductible under Section 170(C)(2) of the Internal Revenue Code of 1986, as amended (or the corresponding section of any future United States Revenue Law.)

AMENDMENT OF BYLAWS

The Articles of Incorporation and these Bylaws may be altered, amended, or repealed, and new bylaws may be adopted by a two-thirds (2/3) majority vote of the Board of Directors of the Church at any regular or special combined meeting of the Board of Directors. At least fourteen (14) days, written advance notice of a meeting called for the purpose of altering, amending, or repealing the Church's Bylaws or Articles of Incorporation shall be given to each member of the Board of Directors.

Adopted by full Board of Directors this _____ day of _____, 20__.

_____
Director

_____
Director

_____
Director

Index

A
Address, headquarters, 126
Advantages, of nonprofit corporations, 23
   Continuous existence, 43
   Employee benefits, 26
   Exemption from labor rules, 23
   Legal life, 26
   Low postage rates, 26
   Right to solicit funds, 24
   Tax exemption, 23
Annual meetings
Annual report
Application for tax exemption. *See Tax exemption, application*
Armed forces organizations in IRS code, 21
Articles of Incorporation 34, 38
See also Certificate of incorporation
   Drafting, 38

B
Benevolent life insurance associations, 20
Black Lung Association, 21
Board of directors
   Selecting, 36
Bylaws, 55
   Drafting, 55
   Sample form, 178

C
Churches, 18, 136
Cemetery companies, 20
Certificate of Incorporation, 33
See also
   Articles on Incorporation, 34, 38
   Disclaimers necessary in, 34
   Drafting, 38
   Sample form, 38
Charitable organizations, 167
   Definition of, 17
   Real estate holdings, 20
Child care organizations, 20
Churches, 18, 136
Conflict of interest statement, 37
Continuous existence, 43
Credit unions in IRS code, 20

D
Directors, 36
   Selecting, 36
Disadvantages, of nonprofit corporations, 29
   Incorporation costs, 29
   Legally required paperwork, 29
   Small operating budget, 30
   Getting outsiders to give. 31
   Disqualifies persons, 37

E
Educational nonprofit corporations, 18
Employee
   Benefits, 27
   Employer Identification Number application, 70

F
Fee payments, 25, 126
Filing fee, 38, 133
Financial reports, filing, 79, 133, 196
Form 8718, 121
Form 872C, 100
Instructions for Form SS4 (application for EIN), 71, 77
Fraternal organizations in IRS code, 20
Funds, soliciting, 24

G-H
Grants, 24
Headquarters address, establishing, 34, 37
Homeowner's associations, 20
Horticultural organization, in IRS code, 20

I
Income tax, on corporations, 23, 153
Incorporating document, submitting, 65
Incorporation
   Advantages of, 23
   Approval, actions following, 141
   Board of directors, waiver of first meeting, 61
   Checklist, 125
   Minutes of board of directors meeting, 55
   Organizational minutes of sole director Costs of Incorporators, 38
Information, by state, 126
Insurance companies, in IRS code, 20
Internal Revenue Service
   8718 form, 121
   872C form, 101
   SS4 Form, 70
   Standards for exemption and tax exemption filing, 169
   Instructions for 1023 form, 175
   Procedural checklist, 125
   8821 form, 79, 175

2848 form, 123
1096 form, 105
1099 form, 141, 157, 165

L

Labor organizations, in IRS code, 20
Legal life, 26
Legal requirements, 29
Liability, 35, 163, 165, 170

M

Mailing privileges, 26
Medical insurance, 19
Membership, in bylaws, 44, 54
Membership organizations, 54
Minutes of meetings, 58

N

Name, selecting, 33
Nonprofit organization, 13
   Advantages of, 23
   Disadvantages of, 26
   Applying for tax-exempt status, 67
   Bylaws, drafting, 55
   Define purpose, 34
   Disclaimers necessary in certificate, 34
   Drafting certificate of incorporation, 38
   Forms (sample), 39, 43, 51
   Headquarters address, 126
   Incorporating document, submitting, 133
   Name selection, 33
   Registered agent, 37
   State fees, 126
   Requirements for Types of Non profits, 17
   How to qualify, 18
   Public/private foundation, 19

Private nonoperating foundations, 19
Private operating foundations, 19
Public charities, 19

O

Officers, 14, 35
Organizational formality, 58

P

Pastors, 193, 195, 204
Postage rates, 25
Private operating foundations, 79, 18
Publications, of nonprofit corporations, 18, 136, 138, 173
Public charity, 18
Purpose, of corporation
   Defining, 34

Q-R

Quorum, 59, 182, 201, 202, 206
Registered agent, 37
Religious organizations, 135
Requirements, for nonprofit corporations
   Arranging for incorporators, 38
   Articles of incorporation, drafting, 38
   Board of directors selection, 36
   Filing certificate and fee payments, 69, 126
   Retirement plans, 27

S

Section 501(C), 17
Self-dealing, 215
Social welfare organizations in IRS code, 19
Soliciting funds, 24
Special-purpose tax exemptions, 19

Annual financial reports, 38
Organizations eligible for
Other categories of section 501(C), 18
Unrelated business income, 69
State information, on corporate laws and forms, 26
Statement of purpose, 34

T

Tax exemptions, 26
   Application, 79
   Advance rulings, 67
   Checklist for completing IRS form1023, 79
   Definitive rulings, 67
   Forms and IRS publications, 71
   Questions from IRS, 97
   Where to send, 142
   Types of organizations exempt, 20
   Teachers' retirement funds, in IRS code, 20
   Telephone company, mutual or cooperative, in IRS code, 20
   Trustees. *See Board of Directors*

U-V-W

Unemployment compensation, in IRS code, 26
Unrelated business, defined, 70, 153
User fee determination letter request, 79
Voting, in bylaws, 36, 57
Waiver of notice, 61, 182

THE BEST GUIDE FOR NONPROFIT CORPORATIONS

WWW.MiracleDeL

Re Maxwell

917 385-9514

93.5 FM Radio
WENSDAY
9PM TO 11PM
PRAYe Line MM
718 9063681